Praise for

I THOUGHT IT WOULD BE BETTER THAN THIS

"If you feel like your loss is too hard, too different, or too big, Jessica Turner is a kind companion. Her advice is hard-won and lived in, blending personal story with practical tools. For anyone in a dark tunnel who can't yet see a light, this book is a candle—a reminder that hope is always an option and redemption may be closer than you think."

—Emily P. Freeman, *New York Times* bestselling author of *How to Walk into a Room*

"Turner knows the brutal heartbreak of unexpected loss and calls upon the reader to keep going, encouraging them to manage expectations, call deep on courage, and to risk embracing change even when it means moving closer to the pain inevitably found inside transformation. This book is a must-read for everyone who has experienced loss and wondered, 'What in the world do I do now?'"

—Meghan Riordan Jarvis, LICSW and author of *Can Anyone Tell Me? Essential Questions about Grief and Loss*

"*I Thought It Would Be Better Than This* offers the calm, gentle wisdom we seek in quiet times. You'll learn to name your experiences and disappointments, grieve them, and find actional steps forward to heal and move on, empowered and clear."

—Tia Levings, author of *A Well-Trained Wife: My Escape from Christian Patriarchy*

"A beautiful, honest, and practical guide for anyone who has found themselves facing unexpected hardships. Jessica's story and hard-won wisdom lets us know we aren't alone and leaves us with hope that even the most challenging things in life can lead us to beauty. A must-read."

—Libby Ward, digital creator (@LibbyWard)
and mental health advocate

"Jessica vulnerably offers a personal but universal guide to navigating life's most painful realities. Both poignant and practical, this beautiful book will help heal your broken heart."

—Katherine Wolf, author of *Hope Heals*,
Suffer Strong, and *Treasures in the Dark*

I THOUGHT IT WOULD BE BETTER THAN THIS

JESSICA N. TURNER

Rise from
Disappointment,
Regain Control,
and Rebuild a
Life You Love

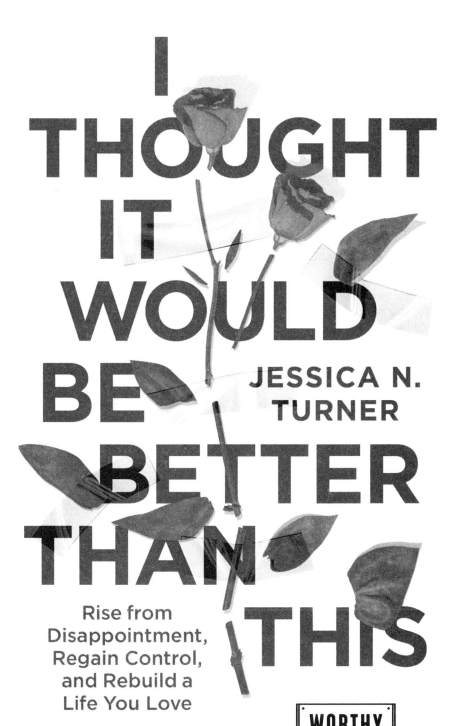

WORTHY
PUBLISHING

New York • Nashville

Worthy Books
Hachette Book Group
1290 Avenue of the Americas
New York, NY 10104
worthypublishing.com
@WorthyPub

First Edition: April 2025

Worthy Books is a division of Hachette Book Group, Inc. The Worthy Books name and logo are trademarks of Hachette Book Group, Inc.

The publisher is not responsible for websites (or their content) that are not owned by the publisher.

The Hachette Speakers Bureau provides a wide range of authors for speaking events. To find out more, go to hachettespeakersbureau.com or email HachetteSpeakers@hbgusa.com.

All Scripture quotations are taken from the Holy Bible, New International Version®, NIV®. Copyright ©1973, 1978, 1984, 2011 by Biblica, Inc.™ Used by permission of Zondervan. All rights reserved worldwide. www.zondervan.com. The "NIV" and "New International Version" are trademarks registered in the United States Patent and Trademark Office by Biblica, Inc.™

Print book interior designed by Bart Dawson.

Library of Congress Cataloging-in-Publication Data has been applied for.

ISBN: 9781546006718 (hardcover), 9781546006732 (ebook)

Printed in Canada

MRQ-T

1   2025

Dedicated to Elias, Adeline, and Ezra.
You will always have my heart.

CONTENTS

I THOUGHT IT WOULD BE BETTER THAN THIS

A LETTER FROM JESSICA

I **didn't appreciate** how easy my life was until I was forced to start over. I was married at twenty-two. I had my first baby at twenty-five, my second at twenty-eight, and my third at thirty-two. My husband was a successful author, and I was a successful business executive with a thriving online business and publishing career. But everything changed when my husband told me he was gay, and we ended our sixteen-year marriage.

The uncoupling process and the trauma of what I experienced, both during and after the divorce, could have led to one of two results: I could have stayed stuck in my sorrow. Or I could rise like the phoenix, the mythical bird who was reborn from its own ashes and has come to symbolize change and growth.

I chose to rise. It wasn't a conscious choice, but looking back, I guess I knew that it really was the only option. If my life was going to have to be made over, I was going to make it better. While I didn't have control over what happened with my marriage, I knew that I had control over how I was going to respond and who I was going to become. I had agency over plenty of my story, and I was determined to be uncompromising in the steps I took to heal. I invested in hundreds of hours of therapy; poured into relationships with family, friends, and new partners; had new experiences; and changed my life. It wasn't a singular moment of saying, "I am not staying in this."

Instead, it was a slow process. The process included taking many steps of going from being broken to soaring, and taking those steps positively affected every single aspect of my life.

I wouldn't wish the pain I went through on anyone, but I believe that it is because of that pain that I have something to offer today. I don't know what your story is or why you picked up this book. But in my eighteen years as a content creator and author, I have received heartbreaking messages from thousands of women in the midst of their own disappointments and battles. Women have told me stories of health challenges, loneliness in their marriages and friendships, unexpected challenges raising children, longings for different careers, sadness in their everyday lives, and so much more. Over and over, I have seen the same aches:

We long for connection.

We long for time.

We long for a dream not yet fulfilled.

We long for something extraordinary amid the mundane.

We long to feel fulfilled instead of disappointed.

We long to be cherished and loved.

In the past few years, in the wake of a painful divorce, I have uncovered each of those longings in myself and have been surprised and encouraged to see many of them fulfilled. It was hard, messy, gritty, and beautiful work. Some days I didn't think I would get to the other side.

In these pages I am going to take you through the steps of my journey so that you might glean from my experiences. I am going to share the tools that helped me rebuild my life when it felt like so much of it had burned down. I hope I don't make it sound like it was easy, because it wasn't—it was the hardest thing I've ever done.

Your story is different from mine, but I believe that many of the methods I used and the wisdom that helped me can help you, too, no matter what you're facing. I found wonderful resources to help me, and it is my hope that this book will become one more resource for you. There is something powerful in someone saying, *Me too. I see you. I understand. Here's one thing to try.*

I believe we all have an innate ability to make our circumstances better, but we so often become too complacent or overwhelmed at the thought of changing direction or investing in ourselves that we stay in the comfort of the status quo. We go about our day, thinking that because this is where we are, this is where we have to stay. When my world was turned upside down, it gave me a blank page to dream, explore, and ultimately say, *I can do things differently—better, smarter, faster, and wiser than I ever thought possible.*

Honestly, if my husband hadn't come out and we hadn't divorced, I would not be the person I am today. I am much more emotionally aware, both of myself and of others. I have a much deeper understanding of trauma and grief and the way those experiences color our lives. I also have learned so much about business and finance. Nearly every area of my life has changed. It seems strange to say that I am grateful to be where I am today because of my divorce, but I am. That forced loss resulted eventually in a lot of good, though it took a lot of pain and work for me to get to a place to say that.

This book is one part memoir and one part self-help, and it is my hope that those two strands woven together will provide a guide for you to navigate your own journey of disappointment. As I wrote this book, I did a lot of research, including reading books on topics surrounding disappointment and growth, interviewing experts, and talking with others who have experienced challenging times. I believe that the combination of stories and practical wisdom, gleaned from my own experiences and research, will allow you to apply the lessons I learned to your own life.

As you read, I encourage you to keep a journal handy. You might find that you want to take notes or journal reflections about your own life and story. You also will find a series of questions and exercises throughout the book that were created to help give you perspective and consider opportunities for change and growth.

Of course, growth and healing experiences aren't served well by a one-size-fits-all approach, but we can take what we learn from different sources and try it on in our own lives. Throughout the book, I will offer stories and ideas for things you can do to aid in your healing and growth. Sometimes the concepts will take some practice—after all, you didn't learn to ride a bike when you first got on the seat and tried to pedal. Likewise, you might find yourself needing to practice what is shared in this book. For instance, I suggest you try journaling. If you have never been a journaler, you might need practice to determine what style is enjoyable and suitable for you and your personality. Or when I talk about therapy, if you have never tried therapy, you might find the experience uncomfortable at first. You might need the practice of attending sessions and opening up to your therapist. Eventually, though, with practice comes strength and knowledge, and knowledge gives us power to change.

I recently was talking with a friend about a challenging situation I was navigating. She said, "You have what it takes to get through it. Just think of who you are now compared to who you were three years ago, when you first got divorced. You are the same, yet completely different."

That is what I want for you. To be the same, yet transformed. To be you, but better, different, and more whole. So many people, when they experience a great loss or disappointment, say, "This happened to me." Period. But I believe that whatever has happened to you is not the end. I want you to say, "This happened to me, *and...*"

This book is the *and*. Bad things happen. Disappointments occur. Dreams are shattered. But those experiences do not need to be the end of the story. You can take control of your life, even in the midst of hardships, disappointments, and failures. Let me share my story and encourage you in yours.

XO,
Jessica

I THOUGHT IT WOULD BE BETTER THAN THIS

CHAPTER 1

WHAT COULD HAVE BEEN BETTER THAN THIS?

"I'm gay."

It was a Thursday morning around seven o'clock, and Matthew, my husband of nearly sixteen years, said the words I didn't want to be true. We stood at the foot of our king-size bed, where we had made love and made babies, where we had confided secrets and dreams. But this was a secret and truth so big that it swallowed me whole. My heart pounded and I could barely breathe.

We'd been in marriage counseling for months, and he had said he was bi just six months before. Since that revelation, we had been wrestling, together and independently, about next steps. Looking back, we were already circling the drain. We loved each other and wanted to find a way forward together. But the force of the water was strong, and the likelihood that we could survive the spiral seemed impossible with this revelation.

"I'm gay, Jess," he said again.

The words came out honestly, but quietly. I could see in his chocolate-brown eyes that he was sincere, sad, and relieved to say those words aloud. They were eyes I knew better than my own. And even in that moment, I loved him. Our three young kids were downstairs, and it was almost time to leave for school drop-off. I can't remember what I said, if anything. I don't remember much of the next hour, but I know that as I tried to drive to work, I felt like I might be having a panic attack. I recall my body shaking as wails erupted from my mouth, though no one was present to comfort me. By eight o'clock I had called in to work saying that I was unexpectedly sick. It wasn't a lie. I was sick with grief.

I came home, walked onto my deck, breathed in a September breeze, and called my friend Jen. I wailed, moaned, and begged for wisdom. But this was uncharted territory, and I knew that no one could advise me on what to do. This would be my own wilderness. I remember thinking, *Maybe this truth would make things easier.* He had told me he was bi in the spring, and our next steps had felt tenuous for months. We didn't know what that meant for our marriage. But if he was gay, we couldn't stay married, right?

A few hours later, Matthew came home.

He sat on the couch and I crawled into his lap, the way a tiny child might. I wrapped my legs around his waist and my arms around his neck, and I sobbed in an unleashed way that I had never experienced. It was primal, deep, and unfamiliar. It was as if my entire body was in the depths of the despair, my howls guttural and full of pain. Matthew held me as I wailed in his strong arms, the ones that brought me comfort my whole adult life. He told me he was sorry and that he loved me. He told me he always would. I sobbed for what was and what was to come. I sobbed because I didn't want to lose him. I sobbed for our kids, for me, and for him. I sobbed because I thought it would be better than this.

MY IDENTITY

My whole adult life, my identity had been centered around the idea of being a wife and working mom. Matthew and I met when I was twenty and he was twenty-nine. We got engaged just nine months after we met, and we married a year later, just a few months after I graduated from college. Our love was fast and deep from the beginning. When Matthew came out to me, we had three children and I worked a full-time social media and marketing job in corporate America. I also had a thriving blog and social media presence, and we had been planning for me to leave my corporate job so that I could do that full time. It was my dream to be an entrepreneur and have more flexibility for my family.

For our entire marriage, Matthew had been a writer, and during the latter half of that career, we had worked together on launching his children's book career. I saw his work as an extension of mine, and it was a joy to help him with everything from brainstorming to marketing. We shared life on social media, did interviews together on podcasts, took vacations as a family, and parented with intention. Our work and life were enmeshed more than the average family, and from the outside, it looked like we had it all.

It's also important to acknowledge right off the bat that I'm a firstborn, type A, Enneagram Type 8, meaning that I am a take-the-bull-by-the-horns leader who likes to be in control. I am extremely capable and fill every day to the fullest. Matthew has often joked that I get more done from five to nine than most people do from nine to five. I love a plan and live and die by my schedule, to-do lists, and goals.

I've always been a planner, and, frankly, divorce was just not part of my plan.

I THOUGHT IT WOULD BE BETTER THAN THIS

Have you ever said that phrase to yourself—or one similar? *I thought it would be better than this.* Chances are, if you are reading this book, you have experienced something in life that went differently from the way you thought it would.

- The loss of a loved one
- The ending of a marriage
- An unfulfilling job
- A health diagnosis
- A financial hardship
- Feelings of loneliness
- Parenting challenges
- An accident or life-changing incident

Any type of *this* is valid. Your story, dreams, and feelings are true and worth articulating. And with those experiences of expecting something different comes an ache for something else. You may be reading this and find you are already very familiar with that ache, or you might have never paid much attention to it. Like people who live in cities with a lot of smog, maybe you don't even realize what life could look like if the skies were clear. Similarly, the smog of disappointment can choke us and leave us desperate for something better. A life that includes unmet expectations and disappointments can create a haze of dissatisfaction that colors your everyday.

Sometimes, the disappointment isn't inherently "bad," but it is different from what you expected and, therefore, still brings up feelings worth acknowledging. I have heard parents say that they thought parenting would be really sunny and happy most of the time, and then they found that it actually is a lot more challenging, frustrating, and exhausting than they expected. I actually never said *I thought it would be better than this* until two years after my husband moved out. I certainly felt it. But when I finally said that phrase out loud, it was as if I had let the genie out of the bottle.

I remember when I first said those words. I was at my friend Lysa's beach house for the weekend. She had invited me and another mutual friend and writer, Ann, to come and talk about book writing. I had shared that I was ruminating on a book idea and would love to flesh out the concept. Lysa and Ann are both accomplished writers, so I valued any insight they could offer. More importantly, they were close friends who had been close confidants during my marriage's unraveling.

We sat on cozy chairs in Lysa's living room, with the sun streaming in and the crash of the ocean's waves creating a soundtrack for the morning. As we talked about the desire in my heart to help other women facing unexpected pain and disappointment in their journey, I said, "I guess I just thought it would be better than this." Ann and Lysa both leaned in, and Lysa said, "That's your book. We all have felt that in our lives."

That simple phrase was packed with so much truth and understanding. It embodied my heart's deepest ache, the unmet expectations I was facing for my love story, my family, and my life as a whole.

As I have processed my own grief and talked with other women about theirs, I realized that this is a universal ache. We have such high expectations for life, but it usually doesn't turn out the way we thought it would. It turns out that we all have our "I thought it would be better than this" circumstances in life. Life is beautiful and messy, and the only thing you can count on is that eventually things will go amok. Disappointment finds everyone. It isn't *if*; it's *when*. And it is what we do when those circumstances arise that makes or breaks us. We can choose to ignore the issue or deal with it just enough to survive, or we can really feel, assess, heal, and grow. The latter takes a lot more work, but it is worth it in the long run.

HOW TO NAME YOUR *THIS*

I can't tell you how many times I have shared the title of this book with someone and their mouth has fallen open, their eyes have widened, or they have simply said, *Holy cow, what a title!* (sometimes all three). I think that is because we have all felt this way. Sure, it might not be your husband coming out that prompts it. It might be that you thought life would look different after being married for twenty years. It might be that you thought you would be in a different place financially at this point in your life. It might be that the trauma you experienced as a child still haunts you. It might be that you thought you would have a lot more friends than you do. It might be that a health diagnosis has radically changed your life in a negative way. It might be that parenting your children is very different from what you imagined. It might be that your work is not fulfilling in the ways you expected it to be. I can't list all the possibilities, but I think you can see that disappointment is both wildly personal and still universal.

Whatever your *this*, it is important to name it so that you can move forward. You can't heal what isn't diagnosed, so being very specific about your pain points can help you heal and thrive even in the midst of hard times. Below, I am going to walk you through an exercise to help you do this. You will discover clarity and be empowered to be more compassionate with yourself and others in the naming and uncovering of your disappointment's layers. It's like an onion. When it is whole, we see a round vegetable, covered in a papery outside layer. There's not much to it. We don't know that it contains so much flavor and so many layers inside. But when we cut into it, that's when we experience its depth—the layers of the onion, its scent, its taste, even the tears it can sometimes cause. Likewise, by doing this exercise, you will be forced to uncover the fullness of your disappointment.

To name your *this*, start by trying to determine the core expectation or ideal that you had. What did you think would be better? Imagine that your core expectation or ideal is the hub of a bicycle wheel. For me, the hub of the wheel was marriage (because I never thought it would end).

Next, consider other related better-than-this expectations extending from the hub like spokes of the wheel. These are other expectations that are unmet because of the disappointment that is the hub. There are no wrong answers here. Consider your core pain points related to your disappointment. It is critical to identify and acknowledge these spokes because they help you understand the breadth of your pain. You will likely have five to ten spokes. For each spoke, use this phrasing: *I thought _____ would be better than this (because _____).*

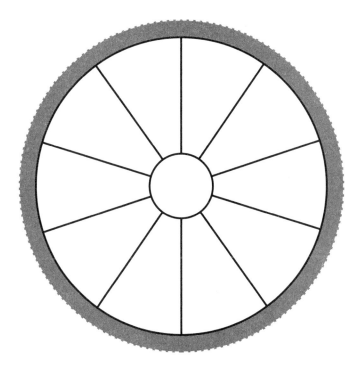

Here are some of mine:

- I thought being loved would be better than this (because I did not expect love to include letting go of the person I was married to).
- I thought forever would be better than this (because I imagined it with only Matthew).
- I thought parenting would be better than this (because I wouldn't be parenting on so many days by myself).
- I thought my financial future would be better than this (because divorce affects finances).
- I thought my forties would be better than this (because I didn't imagine facing them alone and having to start over in so many areas).
- I thought our kids' lives would be better than this (because divorce is painful for everyone).
- I thought my self-worth would be better than this (because it really tanked in the latter years of my marriage and immediately after my divorce).

Depending on where you are in your journey, this process may come to you easily, or you may find it daunting, painful, or too challenging to complete. If you find it too difficult, flag this section and come back to it. I know you will find it valuable, but it is okay to not be able to complete this exercise yet.

If you have completed the exercise, take time to process what your wheel hub is and what the spokes are related to that hub. Are there any themes that emerge? Are there pieces of your pain and disappointment that you have never faced? By acknowledging the breadth of your unmet expectations and pain points, you are able to better discover how to move forward and heal them.

As you process your wheel, have compassion for yourself. It is likely that a lot of feelings will rise up, including grief, frustration, and disappointment. In the forthcoming chapters, I will offer tools to help you define and move through these emotions. Know that you will be able to release hopes and dreams that are unmet or have shifted because of your circumstances. Once you release those things, you will be able to make room for new beginnings and learn from the experiences you have had so far. Releasing something is not forgetting or diminishing its part of your story but rather giving you the freedom to move forward into something new. Sometimes releasing occurs with forgiveness. Other times it occurs when we examine the circumstances that caused us pain. Still other times, it happens through the gift of time apart from the painful experience or unmet expectation. In life, we have the choice to remain bitter and unforgiving or to move forward with forgiveness and compassion for ourselves and others in our story.

THE BEST IMPERFECT CHOICE

After Matthew came out to me, we remained married for a period of time. Matthew didn't want to get a divorce, and I didn't either. We loved each other and also grieved the idea of how divorce would affect our kids and our time with them. Yet divorce was on the table because, even if we loved each other, how could we possibly stay married? Matthew had honestly shared his truth, and staying married felt unfair to us both. We explored the idea of a mixed-orientation marriage, meaning a marriage where people who have different sexual orientations choose to stay married. Some of the questions we grappled with included: Was it enough that I knew that Matthew was gay and that he had shared his truth with me? Could he be happy in a marriage to a woman he loved while also having desires that were unmet because of my gender? Could I be happy, as well?

No one knew what we were going through except for our therapists and a few close friends. We felt it was important to keep this discovery period very private. We didn't need or want to have a bunch of people giving us advice. It would have been too much for us to carry mentally and emotionally, especially when we both were so fragile.

Despite counseling and trying to reconnect as a couple, nothing seemed to be working. Things would be going better for a couple days or weeks, and then I'd notice Matthew turning inward, clearly processing things apart from me. Things were tense, and we were often distant. I battled feeling like I was good enough in every way imaginable. After six months, we decided that we needed to separate. The week Matthew found an apartment, COVID-19 hit and the world shut down. He canceled his lease and we stayed married, living under one roof. I hoped that maybe a pandemic would draw us closer together. I started working from home, and our kids remained home from school. But instead of being one happy family, we were on eggshells constantly.

One spring afternoon, I sat with a wise older friend and said, "I just don't know how to move forward. Every step forward feels like there could be negatives associated with it. How do I know what path to take?"

She gently said, "You must make the best imperfect choice. There are no perfect choices here or in life. Take the information that you have and make the best imperfect choice." She then encouraged me to make a list of my options and what the pros and cons were of each option. Sometimes writing can offer us the clarity we seek in a situation. As I wrote, I saw that no choice was perfect, but the path I needed to choose and the steps I needed to take to get there became clearer.

I have thought about that concept of the best imperfect choice a lot over the past few years. It has become a sage piece of wisdom that I can grab on to when fear or uncertainty grip me. Letting go of perfectionism is freeing. For me, in my story, the biggest, hardest, best imperfect choice was divorce. My marriage became unsalvageable, and as much as I desperately wanted to hold on to the dream of being married for fifty years, of my kids being with me 100 percent of the time, I knew that the best imperfect choice was letting my husband go and starting much of my life over during a season when I thought I would be firmly rooted. I knew that Matthew's freedom to be who he really was would bring freedom to me as well. I don't remember the exact day, but I remember saying to Matthew, with tears running down my face, "I think we need to get a divorce," and the way he slowly nodded in agreement, his eyes filling with tears as well. It was an imperfect choice for us both.

Perhaps in your story you have made imperfect choices or you have some to make. Every area of life requires them. I make them in parenting, my work, my health, and so on. But when an imperfect choice is the result of a disappointment, it often holds more weight. Sometimes, as you move forward with a best imperfect choice, it will feel like the wrong choice. You'll wonder if you should have chosen differently. People will give their opinions, whether you ask for them or not, and you will feel doubt. In these moments, you must trust your gut. Your gut is your guide, there to protect you at all costs. She never steers you wrong. She always looks out for your best interests, and the more you really listen, the more confidence you gain from responding to her quiet whisper of *Yes, you can, this is good* and *No, girl, slow down, think about this*. I knew long before I said "I think we need to get a divorce" that we were going to get a divorce. My gut told me. And perhaps your gut is telling you what to do next as well.

It was late spring of 2020 when we decided that the most loving thing we could do was proceed with divorce and for Matthew to come out to our family and friends. It felt terrifying, but we both had peace about the decision. Matthew's coming out story is his to tell, but I will say that bearing witness to it was one of the most powerful experiences of my life. It was heart-wrenching and heavy to see the person I loved most in the world sharing something that had been so deeply hidden for decades.

In June 2020, Matthew moved out. It was a Saturday. I took our kids to spend the night at a family friend's home, and when I got back to our house (soon to be my house), other friends were there helping Matthew move. It was a somber day. There's nothing happy about seeing objects that were ours become his and hers. I managed to keep a stiff upper lip as the house became emptier, taking my heart with it.

We decided that Saturday evening would be our last night together as husband and wife. We were tired from the move, and though we both liked cooking, neither of us wanted to cook that night. We ordered Outback delivery because a steak dinner, even in takeout containers, seemed like the right choice. We watched a movie. I don't remember what it was, only that it was a mystery/ thriller. I remember lying on the couch with Matthew and thinking that this was the last time he would ever hold me like this. We then went to bed, falling into each other's arms and becoming one for the last time as well. I was surprised that I didn't cry, though I did the next morning when he got up out of bed without showing any affection toward me. No last hug. No last anything. He just got up, like it was an ordinary day. Of course, it wasn't. We both knew it was going to be a terrible day. I think he was likely protecting my heart and his. Why make things harder? I stayed in bed a bit longer, not ready to say goodbye.

A few hours later, after friends had helped him move the big things from my house to his new place, he gathered a few items, getting ready to leave. I went to the garage to put some food from the freezer into a grocery bag for him to have. He met me there and hugged me. I asked if he would kiss me one last time and he gently said, "Of course." He kissed me with a tender kiss that encapsulated love and goodbye at the same time. Thinking about it still makes me catch my breath and tear up. Once in a while I will be in the garage and think about that kiss, as if the ghost of that moment has remained there in that spot.

Matthew's moving out and coming out and our subsequent divorce were the best imperfect choices for us individually and for our family. No choice was perfect, and each would have its own hardship. This is why it took us so long—nearly eighteen months—to go from the time Matthew first spoke his truth to me to finally deciding to divorce. We sought wise counsel, prayed, talked with each other, wept. It was a deeply personal and slow decision.

I don't know what your circumstances are, but my guess is that you, too, are facing or have faced imperfect choices. Life is full of them, but they become more apparent during times of struggle. When life is good, decisions are easy. But when life is hard, you realize that perfection is not possible and that every choice has ramifications. A therapist I saw in this season encouraged me to write lists when I wasn't sure what to do. What were the pros and cons of each choice? Sometimes writing these lists would give me clarity, or at least give me language around my struggles. If you find yourself stuck between two imperfect choices, take pen to paper and write the pros and cons of each choice. Then see if those lists help you make a decision on how to move forward.

When I was a little girl, I used to love Choose Your Own Adventure books. I had a Disney series where the reader got to be a friend of Cinderella, Snow White, and other princesses. In these books there were so many possible outcomes. I loved that each book had so many different stories within it based on the different choices you could make as you read. The hero would face the proverbial fork in the road, and I would pick which direction she would go. The choices were often so ambiguous that you had no way to know if the choice was the right one, but then you'd turn the page and quickly discover if you had made the right choice or not. Sometimes the story would go how I hoped it would, but usually something unexpected would happen. I would think, *Aw! If only I had made that other choice!*

The same is true in life. We are often faced with choices where we make the best decision based on what we know, but sometimes that doesn't mean it is the right one. We simply don't know the ending. We must rely on what we do know and thoughtfully make the best decisions based on our circumstances and what we know in the moment.

WRITE THE NEXT CHAPTER

What I have learned over the past few years is that although we all have seasons when things aren't what we imagined they would be, it doesn't mean that things can't become better than they were before. I truly believe that, and I hope to show you why in the pages of this book.

When my marriage was unraveling, my friend Ann and I would talk regularly about how I was writing a good story, page by page, chapter by chapter, every day. I would call her crying almost every day, and every day she would remind me that I was doing my best to write a good story, to stay present and love my kids, Matthew, and myself, even when it was really hard. To be honest, though, it didn't feel like a good story. Some days it felt like a nightmare. I'm sure Matthew felt the same. This wasn't a story we wanted. It was too hard. Too big. Too raw. Too disruptive to the people in our lives.

But when you think about it, the best stories always have pain and heartache. They are never smooth or easy. We love a hero story that involves overcoming pain, suffering, and difficulties. I think that is partly because we can relate to suffering. Real life is rarely pretty or easy. Also, when it comes to writing a good story for our lives, we can only write our own lines. This was something Ann reminded me again and again when my marriage was falling apart. She would say, "Jess, you can only write your lines here. And you are writing the best story you can, given your circumstances." Others may let us down or force us to take the story of our lives in a slightly (or massively) different direction, but we still hold the pen for our lines.

Another thing about our life stories: they have many chapters. Life constantly evolves and changes. Chapters naturally end and new ones begin. Some chapters are really, really hard. Other ones are easier. Still others seem too good to be true.

The older we get, the more we learn that what we imagine and what ends up happening usually are not the same. If you have said to yourself, *I thought it would be better than this*, then you know this reality firsthand. Our imaginations are rarely right. We have been conditioned to believe that there is magic everywhere, but sometimes life feels pretty far from magical. For me, when I got married, I never could have imagined the pain that resulted from being unexpectedly single after sixteen years of marriage and all that went with that singleness. I met my husband at twenty and barely knew how to be an adult without him. But what I did know, in the weeks that followed, as I sat there in my newly empty house, was that I wanted to thrive and would find my own magic, even though my story hadn't turned out the way I wanted.

My husband's coming out and our divorce was the beginning of something new in my life. When Matthew moved out, I didn't see this new chapter as something to be celebrated. *Oh look! You get a chance to do things over and better!* Um, no. I couldn't appreciate the specialness of the chance to start over because I didn't want it. Looking back now, though, I can see beauty in the way that I was able to find a path forward, discover myself, and do so much I never thought possible. Seeing that time as special now doesn't negate that it was also really hard and something I would not have chosen for myself. This is an important tension for you to embrace as you read this book and endeavor to move forward in your journey.

Things are or will be hard.

Things are or will be wonderful.

Life is a both/and. Think of it like New Year's Day, when the year brims with possibility. You set goals, think about possibilities, and live in the wonder and expectation of what lies ahead. That feeling can be yours anytime, even in the midst of disappointment. I know it's easier for me to write those words than it is to live them. You might be thinking, *You don't know my circumstances.* And you're right—I don't. But it is because I have lived through my own hard circumstances that I truly believe that disappointment can be and often is a catalyst for a sacred beginning.

START YOUR OWN REVIVAL

The three years since my divorce have been like a revival in my life, with so many previously stagnant or dormant areas being brought back to life. I want that for you as well. I want you to know that you have the power to make your story a good one, even if you would have chosen to write the chapters differently. You get to regain control and live in the hope of something better. That doesn't mean that the pain of what you've been through immediately goes away. I still have days when I cry for what was and the dreams that will forever be vapor. But it does mean that you get to harness what you have inside you to make the most of your everyday.

Some might argue that so much of life is what happens to us, and it is what it is, but I think that is a limiting belief. Yes, a lot happens to us that is out of our control. But we still get to choose how we live, in spite of our circumstances. I didn't choose for my marriage to end because my husband is gay. That part of the story was written for me, just like parts of those Choose Your Own Adventure books. But when it came to the parts of the story that I could control, I chose a path that allowed me to lean in to healing, my gifts, and my dreams. It was not easy, but I am glad I forged ahead. In these chapters, you will find tools you can use to help empower you to live the life you desire. But know that you will need to be the one wielding those tools. No one can do it for you.

Oprah Winfrey tells a story about how she was raised in a home without running water and that her grandmother's hope for her was that she would grow up and work for a kind white family. That was her dream for Oprah. But Oprah dreamed different dreams, and not only did she dream those dreams, she went after them. She could have had a life where she was a housekeeper for a family. Instead, she chose a different path. She did not let her circumstances define her. She listened to that small voice that was calling her to greatness.

You have everything inside you that you need to rise above your challenges. You might feel overwhelmed, but take it one step at a time. Lean in to the character traits of commitment, resilience, and perseverance.

Many people choose to be complacent and stay comfortable with the familiarity of what they know instead. Don't be like those people. Reach for something deeper that will last and have a positive ripple effect on your life. Today I can say that I am grateful for what I learned through my divorce, because it allowed me to experience growth and have deeper empathy for those around me. My rose-colored glasses are off, and I now see the ache that many carry.

None of this will be easy, but it will be worth it. On a hard day in 2020, I remember buying a car deodorizer to hang from my rear-view mirror that said "Not to spoil the ending, but everything will be okay." It was a pretty shade of turquoise, and flowers surrounded the words. It was so cheerful and positive during that dark season. I hung it in my car so that every day I would read and cling to those words. Everything will be okay, even if it didn't feel like it that day.

The journey forward is a slow one, and you must take things one day at a time. Be patient with yourself. Have grace when you stumble or a day is hard. This is not a linear journey, but you will move forward if you take even a small step every day. Let me be your guide. I have done this before and I want to walk alongside you. You are worth it.

CHAPTER 2

LIVING THROUGH
THE FIRE OF
DISAPPOINTMENT

Have you ever seen a forest after a wildfire? Our family visited Sequoia National Park in 2021, shortly after a fire had devastated part of the forest. For miles and miles, all we saw were scorched trees, debris, and ash. Instead of the shade of the ancient trees, we saw blue skies, juxtaposed against the blackened trees. It seemed so sad to me—all the death and destruction where tall giants once stood. It seemed like it wasn't supposed to be this way.

When I think about a great disappointment, I think it is like a great fire.

As I shared, Matthew's and my marriage was unraveling during the pandemic. I remember going for a walk one day, desperate to be somewhere other than my home for a few hours. I popped my earbuds in and started listening to *The Complicated Heart Podcast* with Sarah Mae. The episode was called "Processing Trauma with Counselor Adam Young," and it was the first time I had heard someone talk at length about trauma.[1] As I listened to Sarah and Adam discuss trauma and the way it affects people, I realized, *Oh, what I am going through is trauma.* It felt hard and freeing for me to realize that. Hard because I think I thought trauma was reserved for different types of "big" things, like war and assault, and freeing because I now had language to better describe what I was experiencing. According to CrisisHouse.org, psychologists categorize trauma into three main types: acute, chronic, and complex.[2]

Acute trauma results from a single incident.

Chronic trauma is repeated and prolonged, such as domestic violence or abuse.

Complex trauma is exposure to varied and multiple traumatic events, often of an invasive, interpersonal nature.

Other types of trauma exist, as well, but a lot of trauma falls into these categories. While this is not a book focused on defining and unpacking trauma, I think having an understanding of trauma and its potential role in your story is critical for healing. I am thankful for the therapeutic work I have since done related to trauma, as it has given me language and a better understanding of the foundation of some of my responses and behaviors. Trauma is something that most people experience in their lives, regardless of age, gender, or socioeconomic status. In the book *The Unexpected Gift of Trauma*, trauma is defined as "anything that overwhelms a person's ability to cope and to integrate their emotional experience."[3] It is clear to me that most of us—and if you're reading this, this is likely especially true for you—have probably experienced a traumatic event (or events). That event is no doubt part of the burning that you are reckoning with as you read this book.

I love the question posed in the title of Bruce Perry and Oprah Winfrey's book *What Happened to You?*[4] Answering the simple question posed in the title of the book was a game changer for me because it caused me to think about my situation in a new way. I didn't need to just think about what I had done but also what happened *to me*. The "to me" was the trauma, the burning, the experience of losing my husband and my marriage. Your disappointment is what happened to you.

What happened to you? I lost my job.

What happened to you? My mom died.

What happened to you? My childhood was unstable.

What happened to you? _____

I don't know your story, but I do know that you have one. And that story is like that forest I saw: it's burning or burned down. But remember, I didn't see only scorched trees. I saw blue skies. I saw light. There was hope.

Let me tell you something I learned two years after that trip.

In 2023, I was reading a book and learned about the lodgepole pine. It turns out the lodgepole grows in the very park I visited, as well as others. This pine produces a type of pine cone called a serotinous cone, which is closed tightly and covered in a resin that melts only in fire. Sometimes these pine cones will stay on trees for thirty to fifty years. But when a fire occurs, the resin melts, the pine cones open, and they release seeds for new growth after the fire.

Are you taking this in? The forest must *burn* to *grow*. The only way for the forest to flourish is if occasionally a fire comes through and burns the trees to soot and ash. Fire, which can often be perceived as a negative, is actually a positive for the ecology of the forest and the continuation of the species. It is necessary for burning to happen.

This is so extraordinary, and I can't help but think about the analogy for my own life. After the fire of my divorce, I remember feeling so much sorrow. I couldn't see anything but loss and destruction, similar to what I saw when I looked at Sequoia National Park. How could this happen? Where I once saw life and hope in my marriage, I now saw destruction and shattered dreams. The idea of rebuilding, while the fire still smoldered, felt overwhelming. Fire is inherently scary. As children, we are taught to stop, drop, and roll. Fire is bad. It can kill us. We set up smoke alarms to ensure that we get out quickly if a fire starts in our homes. We learn to call 911 and get help immediately. We never, ever want fire. We don't get excited seeing something burn to the ground. Fire means loss. Devastation. Terror.

We aren't usually taught that fire sometimes can be helpful. That it can lead to cleansing and a chance to grow. In all my years of seeing news of forest fires, I don't ever remember a news anchor saying, "Isn't this great to see? Just think about all the pine cones that are going to burst open with new life." But they can. They are. After the fire of my husband coming out and us divorcing, I hadn't yet realized that I was like one of those serotinous pine cones, about to burst open with growth and new life.

My experience isn't uncommon. A friend who was in the midst of a divorce sent me a note that articulated how she thought she had cracked the code on life and that she was going to achieve it all. She got a degree to have a perfect career, married a great guy, and had the perfect family—and then the bottom dropped out. Her husband had been secretly gambling, squandering thousands of dollars, and their marriage ended. She was dismayed that life didn't go how it was supposed to go, and she didn't know why. How was it possible to be in that place, with everything in shambles? She said she had prepared her whole life for success, but no one had taught her how to fail.

When she sent that to me, I thought, *Yes, I remember feeling this way. I thought it would be better than this. I thought life was going to look different, and I was not prepared when things seemingly failed.* Maybe you feel this way, too. These emotions aren't exclusive to divorce. Whatever your circumstances, have you felt like you did everything right, or almost right? You might have. We can do things right and things can still go wrong. You are here, faced with something that is not what you wanted. Your life was supposed to look different. You didn't think the choices you made would lead you here—with everything falling apart.

When I was a kid in the 1990s, one of my favorite shows was *Full House*. Did you watch *Full House*, the show about the widowed dad Danny Tanner whose brother-in-law, Jesse, and best friend, Joey, move in with him to help raise his three kids? When I think back to that show, I recall a lot of hugs and everything always working out. If there was a challenge, a solution was found in approximately twenty minutes. I don't recall any episodes about deep grief, about the blending of these three adults' lives, or about the challenges Danny faced juggling a career and raising daughters. *Full House*'s value statements that good work and kindness will always be enough are reflective of how so many of us were raised—just work hard, be kind, love your family, and everything will always turn out right. Somehow, you'll end up living in a house in a hip part of San Francisco, and if something goes wrong, people will literally upend their lives and move in to help you.

Not true. At all.

It doesn't actually work like that. Death, loss, disappointment, and grief come, and many days you are left to sit in sorrow. You might cry yourself to sleep every night for months, and no one knows. Or maybe you will face emotions and brokenness because no one has ever said "Me, too." You will feel isolated, alone, and bewildered by your circumstances. Why couldn't there have been episodes of *Full House* where Danny cried all day and his kids had to bear witness to the grief and the whole family had to work through it?

What I'm saying is that just because you might find yourself living a life that is different from the lives you saw on television or among your friends, it doesn't mean you did anything wrong. I remember saying to my friend when she sent me that message, "Do you think I did something wrong marrying a man who ended up telling me he was gay after we had three kids? Did I make him that way?"

"No, of course not," she said.

I replied back, "Well, the same is true for you. You made the best decisions with the information you had. You have lived your one beautiful life thus far, and now you are going to keep living with what you know now, in the circumstances that you are in now."

ACKNOWLEDGE YOUR PAIN

During this phase of burning, it is also so important to feel and acknowledge your pain. If you suppress it or quickly move past it, you will continue to be gripped by it. When everything is burning, some of the emotions you might feel include:

- Sorrow
- Anger
- Shame
- Anxiety
- Frustration
- Contempt
- Bitterness
- Jealousy
- Loneliness
- Doubt
- Fear
- Hopelessness
- Disappointment

I remember feeling like every day was Groundhog Day. *When will I stop feeling like this?* I was so tired of crying, of thinking about the future, of going through all the what-ifs in my head. I experienced so many emotions. I felt angry that I wasn't going to be with my kids every day. That was not what I imagined when I became a mom. I felt doubt about how I would manage things that my husband previously had taken care of. I felt fear about the idea of possibly dating in the future. I felt anxiety when I thought about telling our story. And deepest of all, I felt sorrow. How could I step forward in confidence? It was only when I finally made space for those emotions and really processed them—which took a lot of time—that I was able to begin to pull myself out.

You might be wondering, *How do I make space?* Or you might be thinking, *Those feelings take up so much space already! What the heck are you talking about?* Let me tell you more. You see, feelings without action can take root in an unhealthy way. What I mean by this is that if you are feeling something and you never do anything about that feeling, it can overwhelm you. I have learned that the following tactics are helpful for making space for and moving through the pain when things are burning down.

Acknowledge: Notice how you are feeling and the way that feeling is affecting you. Just saying something as simple as "I feel sad today" can bring you comfort. You have a right to feel those feelings, and you should allow them to take up space for a period of time. Sometimes that acknowledgment might also empower you to make changes to your day so that those feelings feel less burdensome. For instance, you might say, "Today, I am really sad, so I am going to go for a walk."

Talk About It: Find someone safe to talk about your feelings with, like a therapist, family member, or friend. Sometimes just taking the time to process what you are feeling will bring relief. I remember once saying to a friend, "I hate feeling needy," and he said to me, "You aren't needy, but it is okay to have needs. It is okay to reach out to a friend and say, 'I need someone to process with today. Can you be that person for me?'"

Comfort Yourself: Think about what you can do to comfort yourself when you are feeling tender. After the divorce, I remember a friend saying, "When you are feeling lonely, what is something else you can do to bring yourself comfort? Can you read a book, write, go for a bike ride?" Do something that will bring you comfort.

Pray: If you believe in a higher power, pray. Crying out to God during times of sorrow helped me cling to the knowledge that someone beyond myself was working on my behalf. If you don't know how to pray, buy a book or download an app that can give you language. You can also light a candle and simply sit quietly, trusting that God hears the aching in your soul.

In chapter 4, I will go into much more depth about these practices.

I think it is important to also acknowledge that some things might never make sense. They just won't. And that is okay. You don't have to have all the answers to move forward and heal. But you do need to make the decision to stop looking back and start looking ahead. If you are constantly looking back, you can't focus on what is in front of you. You also must embrace hope, because hope is like a shield of protection against unknowns and uncertainty in this life.

WHAT ARE YOU DOING TO COPE?

It is also important to pay attention to unhealthy coping mechanisms that you might engage in to stop or numb the pain and uncertainty in your life. These coping mechanisms can play out in a variety of ways, including overeating (especially things like junk food); problem drinking; excessive internet use, gaming, or television watching; sleeping much longer than usual; and overspending (shopping, gambling, etc.). While these mechanisms are not uncommon, they are counterproductive to your healing and growth during this time.

I will sometimes turn to unhealthy foods during times of deep struggle. The consequence is not feeling better, though—instead, I feel sluggish, tired, and crummy. Acknowledging when you are falling into these practices and then making conscious choices to act differently will help you on your journey toward healing. If negative coping mechanisms are something you struggle with, it can also help to engage in accountability with a family member, friend, or therapist to ensure you have the proper support.

STAY PRESENT

When my marriage was unraveling, I kept getting lost in worried thoughts about the future.

I imagined what it would be like to not have my kids with me every day.

I imagined having to start dating.

I imagined Matthew marrying a man.

I imagined being alone forever.

I imagined one million things, even though I had no idea if they would happen.

I also played out what-if scenarios. What if this happened and then that happened and then this other thing happened? Or if it went this way and then that happened and this other thing happened? My mind was always on the future. I was desperately trying to prepare myself for what was to come, but I wasn't preparing at all. Instead, my worrying was causing anxiety, heartache, frustration, and more sorrow.

Worrying can wreak havoc. In the book *What's Here Now*, Jeanne Stevens brilliantly writes, "The language of worry consumes itself in the not yet as it looks beyond the now. Worry sweeps away today's happiness by rehearsing tomorrow's headaches. It gets us stuck in possible problems. And when we are run-down and overwhelmed it's rarely our hard work that causes our frustration and resentment—it's our worry. Worry is simply living in a not yet that is worse than your now."[5]

My therapist would tell me again and again to stay present. She would gently remind me, "You don't need to worry about that yet. Right now you need to focus on today, tomorrow, this week. You don't know what is going to happen."

During this time I found the song "One Day" by Christa Wells. The chorus of the song says to move through your days one at a time, sometimes literally one breath and one prayer at a time. I would do my best to sit with Christa's words, reminding myself that I was doing it. One day at a time. That doesn't mean I didn't still get stuck in the traps of worry, but I slowly found myself shifting into more present thinking instead of future thinking.

My friends also helped with this. In one of my favorite children's books, *Ruby Finds a Worry*, the little girl Ruby has a worry that is like a little monster cloud, always hovering in the shadows.[6] It gets bigger and bigger until she finally says the worry aloud. Once she speaks of it, it loses its power over her and gets smaller. Like Ruby, I learned that sometimes I just needed to say the worry aloud, and then someone else could help me hold the fear and let go of it.

Living in the present was one of the greatest lessons I learned in the burning. These days, when someone comes to me and shares their disappointment, they often will start their own list of what-ifs. I will gently say, "I know how you are feeling. I remember having a bunch of what-ifs after Matthew came out. The best advice I can give you is to stay present. If you find yourself jumping ahead, gently redirect to right now. You can't know all the answers just yet. They will come. And when they do, you will be ready. For now, stay focused on what you can do about what is right in front of you. Keep doing that."

BEAUTY CAN COME FROM ASHES

When my friend sent me that message saying that she expected her life to be perfect after doing all the "right" things, I wrote back to her, saying:

> Life isn't like this. Nothing about it is perfect. It is messy, and things burn down. But beauty can still rise from ash. In fact, in my experience beauty comes from the rising. It is easy to thrive when everything is easy, but when everything falls apart, how will you live? What choices will you make? Will you only look backward, or will you look ahead? You have the opportunity to begin again. What you're going through is not what you wanted or expected, but it is your life today. Do not live in a state of resentment for what is not. Instead, live with the motivation to create something beautiful with what you have. You are so fortunate. You have assets, talent, and, most importantly, kids who adore you. You have a big heart. The code is not perfect job, perfect house, perfect family. The code actually has nothing to do with perfection. The code is this: Live wholeheartedly. Let love in and flourish. Forgive. Count your blessings every day. These are the things that will change your life.

Once I went through my own burning, my eyes were opened to the pain that so many people are walking around carrying. It was sobering to face the reality of so much pain. Everyone has something that is hard, and most people are not talking about it. Before, I knew people experienced pain, but I am ashamed to say I didn't really understand the weight of it. Now I see pain everywhere. We are all walking around with a heavy load, and it is the way we choose to live through it that allows our lives to be ones of renewed joy or continued sorrow.

I read in an article that after one Yellowstone forest fire, "ninety-five percent of these trees [growing in the area that was burned twenty years earlier] germinated in the first year after the fires."[7] I don't think we humans are as good at growth after fire as that pine tree forest. Some of us get used to the fire to the point that we will just continue to let things burn versus making the choice to slough off that layer of wax and bloom. I've known people who stay bitter, who don't forgive, who continue to live life in ruin instead of making the active choice to build again. In Mike Mariani's brilliant book *What Doesn't Kill Us Makes Us*, he writes, "Catastrophes do not trigger transformation; they only establish the conditions that increase the likelihood that we will pursue them. Only through our willful, persevering actions can we gradually remake our identities."[8] We humans are not like pine cones, because we have free will. We get to choose whether to stay closed or to open. It will be hard to open yourself up to growth and change, but I hope you will do it anyway. You have one life and deserve for it to be as full and vibrant as you imagine.

I recall at one point saying to someone, "I feel like I am lying on the floor of hell and everything is burning." I felt parched, burned, and hopeless. Sometimes the fires of life are a slow burn like a forest fire, while others are like an explosion. In both cases, though, the result is devastation and ash. That devastation requires a massive cleanup. Things must be torn down, dismantled, and carried out. The same is true for a disappointment. The first step is often a dismantling. You will have to work through and carry out things that are no longer true, valid, or working. And after that burning and dismantling comes the necessity of building something new or different than before.

This work is significant and will require resilience. When everything was burning for me, it was difficult to see beyond the fire. I didn't give credit to my resilience to not just survive the initial shock of my divorce and my loss of life as I imagined, but to actually build back better. Resilience is that fortitude. When you're in it, it is difficult to see that strength, but you have it. We are born with it. Every day in those first few rough years, I would remind myself that the only way through was through. In fact, the journey I was on was not one of climbing out of a pit but of walking through a tunnel. Eventually, I trusted I would find light again, even when things seemed so dark. Because sometimes the tunnel is *really* long and you can't see the light, even though you know it must be there.

It takes courage to move forward when the world around you is smoldering. Sometimes it is hard to believe you have courage when what you mostly feel is fear, sadness, ache, and loneliness. I know that. I remember. But looking back, I had so much courage. And so do you. Reach for it. Take a deep breath. And let's take the next step toward healing.

CHAPTER 3

SPEAKING THE WORDS YOU MOST FEAR

When I was a little girl, my favorite movie was *Anne of Green Gables*, starring Megan Follows. Many *Anne of Green Gables* literature fans are passionate about this movie version, and I am no exception. Don't come at me, Netflix *Anne with an E* fans!

Anne is an orphan with a big imagination and flair for drama. There is a scene in the movie where Anne has lost her best friend, Diana, because of a misunderstanding with Diana's mother. Anne is talking with her teacher, Miss Stacey, as they walk on a path lined with trees, and Miss Stacey counsels her with wisdom from the Bible, saying, "In the end, the truth will set you free." This gives Anne the resolve to keep going forward with the hope that her friendship will be restored when the truth is revealed.

This scene with Anne and Miss Stacey is one that I think about often because I have seen this play out again and again in my own life. The truth does set us free. Keeping things hidden never serves us well. But when it comes to a disappointment, getting to that freedom can feel daunting because oftentimes the ripple effect of telling the truth can be negative—at least at first.

WHY WE FEAR TELLING

Speaking aloud our disappointment and pain is inherently risky. Admitting to something that has gone differently from how you dreamed it would comes with a lot of weight. I remember thinking for months about how it would feel to say things like:

- My marriage isn't what you think.
- We've been unhappy for years.
- Matthew is gay.
- We are getting a divorce.

While your disappointment in life is probably different from mine, I bet the pit you feel in your stomach over the idea of saying that disappointment aloud feels the same. I bet you might worry about the ramifications, those gnawing feelings: *I don't want to do this. How will they react? This isn't good.* We can get caught up in the what-ifs, worrying about how people will react and what will happen after we say the words. These thoughts often prevent us from stepping out. The barriers to truth-telling are vast. Some of the reasons that we might choose to not tell the truth include:

- We have gotten comfortable with the status quo, even if it is unhealthy, painful, or less than what we want for our lives.
- We are afraid of how others will react.
- We are trying to protect people we love from getting hurt.
- We are concerned about the cost (financially, mentally, socially, etc.).
- We are ashamed of the truth.
- We want to avoid more disappointment.

I understand all of these barriers, and I am here to tell you that none of them are worth continuing to live from a place of *I thought it would be better than this.* Telling the truth is your path toward freedom and new beginnings. I know this because I lived it. The truth about Matthew's sexual orientation and our subsequent divorce was a scary thing to share, both in private circles and publicly. At one point, we debated whether to tell people the reason when we announced we were getting a divorce. I wanted him to come out because I knew the secret would continue to be a burden if he didn't say it out loud, but he was very nervous about the negative personal and professional consequences that might result.

The biggest reason why he did not want to come out was because he was afraid of how his family would react. His family is extremely theologically conservative and not LGBTQ affirming. At one point he said to me, "Jess, I am afraid I will cause my dad to have a heart attack." I believed that his family would love him and embrace him no matter what, and he felt certain things would change between them. But Matthew knew that the truth was the only way to move forward. He bravely told his parents and sisters that he was gay, and they did not react well. Since that time, they have essentially severed their relationship with him and our family. It is one of the most excruciating losses of our lives.

Publicly, we were also "canceled" by many people who unfollowed us and stopped reading our writing and sharing our work. Websites wrote about us without knowing anything about our story. People called us horrific names on social media and made callous remarks. The judgment we feared did happen, but it was not bigger than the freedom that we found in stepping out in truth.

My husband coming out to me, then to his family and friends, and then to the world set him free emotionally. I saw him come back to life in the months that followed. I also experienced relief, because

I had thought many of the problems in our marriage meant there was something inherently wrong with me and my body. I'll tell you more about that later, but I wrote many narratives in my head of why things didn't seem like I thought they should, but they all were false. It turned out our disconnect was about Matthew's secret, not about me. The freedom we experienced after we told people what was going on didn't make the truth any less devastating. Of course it was terrible. It meant our marriage ended, our kids lived in two homes, his career as a Christian writer was affected, and his family was no longer a part of our lives. I'm writing this four years later, and it still makes me cry to think about that time. It was so hard.

Admitting that life is not what you imagined it would be is difficult. That cost of stepping out in that truth might feel so great that you might feel safer staying in the shadows. I know this is how Matthew felt. But secrecy has a cost, too. And secrecy is like black mold, spreading its toxic chemicals into the air as long as it exists. Black mold can destroy everything. In homes, the walls will sometimes need to be ripped out completely if black mold is found. Likewise, a secret can cause destruction in many ways. So how do we go about approaching the truth, navigating the hard parts, and finding that freedom that we desperately desire? Here are six actions you can take that may help you have the courage to speak up about your disappointment.

Action 1: Start Therapy

I had never been to therapy prior to my marriage unraveling. Five years later, I can honestly say it was one of the best things to come from this period of my life. I think for many of us, when we don't know who to tell or we don't feel safe to tell anyone, engaging with a therapist is the perfect way to begin.

When Matthew and I were married, we were on a tight budget, so I found a practice that had therapists in training with modest rates. Matthew and I saw a couples therapist as well as individual therapists. Though our therapists were just beginning their careers, they offered wisdom, understanding, and safety during a period of great uncertainty.

I want to note that it is important to find a therapist who suits you well. This is not someone to settle on. You know yourself best, and you can discern if a therapist is good for you and your circumstances. Our first couples therapist was not a fit for us. I'll never forget when he suggested that we try having an open marriage. While we wanted to remain married, Matthew and I were not willing to compromise on the vows we had made to each other. His suggestion made me feel like he was not listening to who we were or what we wanted, and I especially did not feel emotionally heard and safe, as I felt like his suggestion was trying to be helpful for Matthew and not me. We quickly moved to another therapist in the practice that was a better fit.

My therapist was Stephanie, a tall woman about my age with big doe-like eyes and long blond hair straight out of a shampoo commercial. She has a spirit that is both gentle and resolute, wise and kind. Finding her during this season is a grace I'll never get over. From the moment I met her, I liked her and knew she would hold the fullness of my emotions with respect and dignity. During one of our first sessions, we sat in a room that was about the size of a closet, with cheap-looking modern furniture and a small lamp that cast a comforting glow in the space. As I told her where things were with Matthew and our marriage, I cried my eyes out. I remember the pile of wet tissues next to me, sitting there as a physical representation of the depth of my sorrow. And then, I looked up, taking a breath from my story, and noticed that Stephanie's eyes were glistening with tears, too.

I don't remember exactly what she said, but I think it was something like, "Your sadness is appropriate. You will get through this."

What I do remember is that her bearing witness to my story, during that period when literally no one else knew what we were walking through, gave me courage to keep going. Her tears made me feel safe. This was a woman who was bringing her humanity to her practice, and that was such a gift. I also remember feeling so much less alone.

This is what telling does. It makes us feel less alone. And when we feel like our thing is too big, too confusing, or too much to share with others in our life, therapy is a safe place to begin. It is an opportunity to uncover and discover what we are feeling, what we need, and how we should move forward when we are faced with turmoil, disappointment, confusion, and suffering in a nonjudgmental, healing space. Therapy also helps us see blind spots in ourselves and our situations. It is an act of dignity for yourself to sit in the discomfort of having a therapist call those things out.

In the months and years to come, it would be Stephanie who would sit with me, week after week, month after month, as I navigated grief, created new systems for my life, and developed courage to rebuild things from the ground up. Therapy is a sacred space for people to process without judgment and heal as slowly as they need to. It is an opportunity to learn about yourself and the way you move in the world. And it is an opportunity to speak aloud things that you have only ever carried alone.

When you don't know what to say or how to say it, therapy is a good place to begin. You will discover the language you need to share your story and feelings.

Action 2: Invite Others In, but Start Small

In Brené Brown's book *Atlas of the Heart*, she outlines grief and writes that telling our stories is part of healing.[1] It is true that it is impossible to heal and grow if we don't speak about what we have experienced and are going through. You must invite others in to heal.

When our marriage was burning down, I needed people to know. But I also felt like I couldn't tell most people I knew in the midst of it because I couldn't carry the weight of their processing, grief, and sorrow. I didn't even tell my closest family members because I knew that then, in addition to my own suffering, I would have to navigate theirs as well. I couldn't answer questions or attempt to carry their own pain about our difficult situation yet. It was a challenging decision, but my heart was so fragile, and I knew I had to protect it.

When you are thinking about who to share your story with, consider the following:

- Is this person safe and trustworthy?
- Will this person gossip about me and my circumstances?
- Do they have the bandwidth to be there for me during this season?
- How will it feel to tell them?
- Will they react in a way that is helpful or hurtful?
- How much wisdom can they bring to this situation?

By honestly answering these questions, you will gain clarity about who to invite into your story.

After several months in therapy, I decided to tell a few close friends about Matthew and what was going on in our marriage. I needed more people to know. I was too fragile to keep carrying this massive secret on my own. My friend Ann, in particular, was my go-to. I called her nearly every morning on my way to work, usually crying. She gave me the gift of "withness," literally being with me through every day of sorrow. I remember the drumbeat of her words, helping me to see bits of light when my eyes could only focus on the dark. I couldn't bear to be alone in the secret for more than twenty-four hours, so calling Ann every morning helped get me through. I think creating that rhythm of speaking the day's pains, heartaches, and truths to Ann helped me survive those dark days. Though every day was painful, navigating them with someone helped me feel like I would be okay.

Through this process I learned that truth-telling is often a slow, one-on-one endeavor. If you are dealing with a disappointment, identify one person or a few people you want to let in first. This keeps it manageable. Eventually, you might become more comfortable with broadening that network of people, but don't feel like you need to articulate your hard thing with many right away.

Action 3: Talk About Your Pain

Depending on your situation, you might be okay with talking about your problem, but it still may be difficult to talk about your pain related to it. For instance, if you are facing a difficult financial situation, you may find it easy to talk about the nuts and bolts of the situation but difficult to talk about your suffering that has come with it.

Matthew coming out was widely celebrated, as it should be. His deepest truth was no longer hidden, and he was now able to live fully in his identity in a way our marriage didn't allow. In the months after Matthew told me he was gay, I encouraged him to come out to his family, his friends, and the public. I loved him so much, and I wanted to fully support him. I found it easier to talk about our divorce and the why than to talk about the pain I was feeling.

About a year after he came out, a male acquaintance reached out to me and said he'd love to chat. He was gay and had come out a few years earlier. We had some mutual friends, and I respected him, though I didn't know him well. On our call he said to me, "I just want you to know, you have been very brave and honorable in the ways you have celebrated Matthew, but I know that you must be suffering a lot. You don't talk about it a lot because I think you fear that sharing your pain would cast a shadow on the positivity of Matthew coming out."

I was gobsmacked by how meaningful his acknowledgment was to me, and I told him so. I felt like if I talked about how painful it was to learn that my spouse was gay, about the dissonance between what I'd experienced in my marriage and this new truth, about my body image and how this new fact had colored everything, I would be causing pain to Matthew. And I didn't want to do that.

For a long time, I kept my pain mostly to myself because I didn't want to cause more harm to Matthew. I saw his suffering more than anyone else. But that quietness was causing harm to me.

Slowly, I began to really articulate my pain. I began writing about my loneliness, my ache, and my sorrow. I felt more freedom to share my story with people close to me and publicly online.

Remember, two things—even two things that are opposing in nature—can be true at once. Matthew could be celebrated *and* I could be suffering. There could be destruction *and* freedom. Matthew could be brave and happy to be living out his orientation, *and* I could be incredibly sad that the marriage and partnership I had expected to have all my life was no longer possible.

To fully move forward, it is important to pull back the curtain on all your feelings. When you talk about them, they cannot maintain the same strong hold on you that they have when they are held in secret. It prevents them from growing roots and causing resentment.

Action 4: Write Your Story

You don't have to consider yourself a writer to write your story. Writing is a powerful action for releasing what you are thinking, feeling, and experiencing. I would journal at different points during this period, and the simple act of getting my experiences down on paper helped me to feel that I was not alone. If you have never been a journaler, it is not too late to begin. A few approaches you might take:

- A paper journal, where you freewrite about your day, your experiences, and what you are feeling
- A private Google Doc, where you can type your experiences
- A guided journal that offers daily prompts
- Letter writing, where you write letters to yourself, either in present tense or to your future self

I will discuss journaling in more detail in chapter 11.

Action 5: Embrace the Messy

Along with acknowledging your pain comes a lot of messiness. Whatever disappointment you face, it likely comes with emotions that are hard and messy. Give yourself permission to feel those feelings, and be willing to share them with others. You do not have to always keep yourself together for the sake of those around you. Let yourself get raw. Cry. Scream. Sleep. Yell. Whisper. Write. Pray. Run. Walk. Sit. No one singular formula exists to get you through, but you will get through. Be gentle with yourself during this process.

I have had moments when all I could do was cry and cry and cry. I've sat in my bed and wept over the moments I'd never have, the dreams shattered, and the ache that life was just not supposed to look like this. I've felt pain deeper than I could have imagined possible.

I remember calling my friend Angie and sobbing over the grief of the fact that this was my story. It was what felt like the hundredth call to her like this. Through my snot and tears, I said, "I'm so sorry that you have to keep sitting with me in this." I remember feeling like my constant sorrow was a burden for my friends to help me carry. She shut me down so fast, saying, "Never say that to me again. It is a privilege to love you and be with you in this."

Other times, I would throw myself into work, sometimes working fifteen to eighteen hours a day, using the work to push aside my grief. I would work at night with my laptop in bed, literally until I could hardly hold my eyes open. Then I would wake up and start working again, from the same spot in bed. I put energy into building a new dream instead of wallowing in my loss. This excessive work wasn't sustainable in the long term, but it helped me during that season to shift some of my attention into something new that was life-giving.

The problem is, we have been sold an ideal about life that is not real. We think we are supposed to be perfect and present ourselves as whole, together people. This is why I felt like I needed to apologize to Angie for crying. The truth is, my sorrow didn't make me less whole or less together. Rather, it added to the depth and richness of my story and who I am.

The only thing that is certain is that life will not go according to plan. In the Tony Award–winning musical *The Outsiders*, the main character, Ponyboy, goes through a sequence of traumatic events. His parents die in a car accident. His best friend dies. A fire happens in his town. He sings a song called "Great Expectations" about how he had so many expectations for life and none of them have come true for him. We see him near the end of the show, shell-shocked with grief. His brothers try to encourage him to go back to school. They spur him on, saying that they lost their parents and they could not lose him, too. They love him. And though the show ends shortly after their encouragement, we know that Ponyboy does begin to pick up the pieces of his life and move forward.

We all have moments like Ponyboy had when we are faced with the reality that our great expectations have turned into unmet expectations. When life doesn't go according to our plans, we get to decide if we are going to live with our current circumstances, or if we are going to lean in to seeking clarity to make them better. Pony-boy's circumstances certainly lent themselves to making it easy to stay in that vortex of sorrow, but that pain was not sustainable. He had to do better for himself. He had to fight for healing.

It is possible that your life has been a certain way for so long that it feels scary to admit to your dissatisfaction. And in fact, being honest might make things messier, at least at first. But living a happy, fulfilling life means not sweeping things under the rug or pretending that good enough is good enough. You get one life and one chance to make your life beautiful.

It's kind of like when you decorate for Christmas and at first it is a big mess. You get out all the boxes and then starting opening them, creating more havoc as bunches of lights, piles of tissue paper, and knickknacks make their way out of the boxes. But slowly, you find places for everything. The lights get strung on the tree. The garland is wrapped around the porch railings. And the nativity set is laid out again. Instead of chaos, you feel peace. As the tree twinkles, you realize that the mess was worth it. In life, sometimes you have to make a mess and speak your truth before things can get better.

Action 6: Seek Out Expert Guides

I have already talked about therapy, but the experts I am referencing here are other service professionals who can guide you as you change course. For a long time, I found that my pride prevented me from asking for help. I thought I should know how to do things or be okay with the status quo of whatever I was doing. But then I realized I needed to ask for help in areas where I didn't have enough knowledge or experience. The same is likely true for you. For instance:

- If you are looking to change jobs, talk with a career coach.
- If you need financial counsel, talk with a financial planner.

- If you need help managing your home, hire a professional cleaner or organizer.

In my experience, having people with niche experience enter your life gives you freedom to grow, learn, and change in ways that were previously impossible.

For these professionals to do their best work, you have to be vulnerable. You have to be willing to confess the things that haven't gone right or that you have been ignoring. I realized after my divorce that I needed a lot of wisdom around the finances of my business, which my husband had previously handled. I networked and found an accountant and a financial planner to help me. I knew I couldn't do it on my own, and it was very vulnerable to say, "I don't know these things; can you please help me?" Over time it got easier and I became empowered. I honestly think that had I not sought out professional help, I wouldn't have experienced the growth in my business and my financial security as quickly as I did.

Of course, getting expert help doesn't have to be costly. You could network with friends, reach out in Facebook groups, or use the library. The point is, part of changing the trajectory of your story is seeking out help from people who know more than you do.

YOU'RE NOT THE ONLY ONE

The unexpected benefit of telling your truth is that you will likely discover others in your community walking through similar circumstances. You might also empower others to tell their truth.

The Monday after Matthew moved out, I was on a conference call for work about Pride Week. One of my colleagues, Jo, said, "I am probably one of the most affirming people on this call because a decade ago, my husband came out." The color drained from my face as I realized that this woman, whom I respected very much, intimately knew the intense pain I was currently facing.

After the call, I reached out to her, shared my story, and asked if we could talk. She became a safe confidant, and I reached out to her periodically as I walked through transition after transition. She was always just a text or phone call away, and knowing that I could rely on her brought me great comfort. In writing this section, I scrolled back through our texts and found so many like this one: "Wishing you peace, strength, patience, and joy in the discovering of this new adventure. Be sure to listen to your inner voice. Sending you hugs and love."

In my time of sorrow, I wouldn't have used the word *adventure*, but having Jo there to tell me that it would be an adventure gave me hope. Her perspective and steadiness were calming graces to me. When you find others in your circle who can offer wisdom because they have been there, too, allow them in. Trust their voices to offer perspective and hard-won truth.

I have since become that confidant for other women walking a similar path to mine. It is a privilege to offer hope, courage, and wisdom for women navigating a spouse coming out, divorce, or leaving a job. Whatever your story is, trust that you are not alone in it and that sometimes your willingness to share will bring hope to someone else.

FREEDOM FROM PAIN

For three generations, the women in my family have gotten hysterectomies around age thirty-eight. My nana. My mom. And then me (one month before I turned thirty-eight). Genes are wild, right? For me, the surgery came after dealing with endometriosis for years, along with painful periods and cysts. I put it off for more than a year, feeling like it was better to keep managing the pain and other symptoms rather than deal with a major surgery and recovery.

It got to a point where I could not put it off any longer. After I had the surgery, the recovery was slow and hard. It took months to heal. But eventually I did, and I couldn't believe how much better I felt. It was life-changing. I was like a new person. So many areas of my life were better because I wasn't dealing with constant pain. I realized that often we live with pain for so long that we can't even fathom life without it.

My hysterectomy is a reminder that when we finally deal with our pain, freedom is found. A huge part of that process is speaking up and sharing our stories. You might be in a season where everything is painful, uncertain, frustrating, or just plain disappointing. And telling the truth, like my surgery, will cause more pain. Yet in time, you will be better. Life will be better. You just have to take that next step of going to the doctor and saying, "I need help. Something is wrong, and I want a better life."

CHAPTER 4

EXPLORING YOUR GRIEF

Along with the burning and truth-telling comes grief. Whatever your disappointment, your pain is going to journey with you throughout this book and throughout the process of your healing. That is inevitable, and that is okay. I wanted to acknowledge grief early in this book because I don't want you to think that grief has not been a companion to every good thing I share in the chapters to come.

In fact, I think it is because of my grief that I mustered the courage to move forward. I knew I didn't want to sit in the valley of sorrow forever. When we hold on to a grief-only story, we become bitter, angry, and resentful. It becomes like a poison, slowly changing our worldview, making our relationships toxic, and sucking the life out of us. I have watched this happen in other people, and I knew that I did not want to live that way. So I chose a path that included grief as *one* of many emotions in my story.

As I touched on earlier, I deeply believe in an *and* life, where two things can be held simultaneously. I don't believe that you can be only happy or only sad. I believe that you can experience great joy *and* have sorrow. I believe you can make beautiful memories *and* wish you had someone to share them with. I believe you can thrive in a job *and* mourn a career that you lost. Life is filled with so many *and*s.

In January 2024, three years after my divorce, Nashville was hit with a big snowstorm. We got eight inches, which was double what we usually get in a year, in just one day. Matthew had been at my house the day before the storm, but the day of the storm, he remained at his house and I was at mine with our kids. The kids and I had a great day sledding, making cocoa, and enjoying a fire, but it was also a hard day for me. I kept thinking about my life as a divorced mom and how things used to be. I thought about how much I missed having a husband to share in the fun and the work. I felt really lonely. It was a day of *and*s. Fun memories. A lonely heart. Both were valid and both were true. I felt the absence of having a partner, and I grieved that. I've learned to acknowledge grief when it pops up, so I did so that day.

By embracing the *and*s of life, you are able to move through things more fully. You become in tune with your heart's yearnings, desires, and delights. This may be challenging, though, if you are caught up in the lies of grief.

GRIEF IN THE BEGINNING

I don't know where you are in your story, but if you are in the early stages of disappointment, it may feel like grief is swallowing you whole. I remember feeling like a shell of a person in the days after Matthew came out to me. I couldn't eat, sleep, or work. I went through the motions of my day, without the capacity to really pay attention to what I was doing.

While I knew that life included disappointment and heartache, it wasn't until my husband's coming out and our divorce that I really was faced with the depth of what grief does to you. It is strange to me that we are taught so many things in life, but we aren't taught how to handle disappointment and grief. Those who have experienced it nod with understanding, but why aren't we all taught about grief's impact and how to live after in the same way we are taught history, math, and science? I felt so alone and unsure of what to do. During that period of deep grief, my head and heart became an echo chamber of sadness, confusion, heartache, and doubt. I was so, so sad. It was as if I were Jonah and the grief was the whale, swallowing me whole. Grief, especially in the beginning, is hard because it is all-consuming and painful. You might also not be willing or able to share about it yet, which, as I wrote in the last chapter, makes things even harder.

I recall standing in the kitchen at my office, where my colleagues were drinking coffee and talking about their latest Netflix binges. I wanted to scream, *Must be nice to have a normal life! My husband is gay and everything is falling apart!* But instead, I'd nod my head and smile, hiding what was choking my own life.

It was like I was living two lives: the life that people saw at work and on the internet, where everything was fine, and the life I lived when I was in my home and alone, where absolutely nothing was fine. The tension of living both of these two realities was brutally difficult. Given the circumstances, I don't know that another way was possible, but I can see now how much it added to my grief. By the time we decided to divorce and Matthew came out, I had been sad for so long that actually being able to talk publicly about the sorrow made it a little easier.

If you are in the early stages of grief, what they say is true—it does get better. I know it is easier said than lived, but I promise, you won't stay here. You must keep moving ahead, trusting that there is a way out of the cavern of disappointment. Believe that this is not where you are meant to live, and fight for hope, even when it all seems hopeless.

THREE LIES ABOUT GRIEF

We have been taught several lies about grief. The first is that grief is something you get over. This is simply not true.

Lie #1: Grief Has an End Point

I used to believe that grief was a journey that had an end point when someone would be "better." I know now that this is not how grief works. Grief is not something to get over. There aren't five simple stages to complete. You don't get a gold star and get to never be sad again. In fact, grief doesn't have an end point. It is a forever companion in life. Once you experience deep grief, it changes you and is always with you. It does evolve over time, and joy can and will take residence again in your body, but it will sit on the shoulders of grief and its impact.

Grief lingers for a lifetime. The scars and wounds that mark our minds, bodies, and souls are always with us. And no matter how "healthy" you get, you will still be informed by the painful moments you have experienced. This doesn't mean that life is always going to be sad or difficult, but rather that the dimension of grief is simply one of the many emotions we carry with us.

Four years after my divorce, I had a conversation with a friend about something that had bothered me in my marriage. All of a sudden, I got very emotional, my eyes welling with tears as I spoke. I took a breath and said, "Gosh, I guess that is a wound that hasn't fully healed." It was a reminder to me that gentleness with ourselves must be a part of the way we live after grief.

Lie #2: Your Grief Is Too Much for Others

Another lie that we have been taught is that our emotions can be too big or too much for others to handle. We see people in the media and in our own lives presenting experiences that are "perfect," or at least everything seems "fine." This makes it difficult to believe that our "not fine" lives are going to be welcomed by others. What I have learned is that everyone has hard parts of their stories and we do not need to be quiet or shy about our pain.

In fact, the more authentic, honest, and vulnerable we are, the more others can relate to us. For a long time, I didn't want to tell the truth about my story because it felt too hard, too different, and too big. But then, as I told people about what was happening, I realized it wasn't any of these things. Every person I told helped lighten my load by carrying a piece of it with them. Moreover, I was surprised by how many people could relate to my story, even if it was different from their own.

Lie #3: Grief Should Be Hidden

Another lie is that grief should be kept hidden. I have a friend who went through a painful season of multiple people in her life passing away. I would periodically call her to check in and she was always taken aback that I remembered her grief. I think most of the people in her life had assumed she was doing "fine," though she was still filled with much pain and sorrow. She would often put on a happy face and move through her days, instead of feeling free enough to say that things were still hard.

Grief is not meant to live in the shadows. It does best in the light, where others can see it, hold it, and help carry it. Grief is too heavy to carry alone. Do not believe the myth that your story cannot be shared or that the ramifications of your sorrow are too much. It is not true. Grief eventually enters everyone's stories, so believe that others can join you, right where you are.

SIX STRATEGIES TO NAVIGATE GRIEF

When I was in college, I went boating with a group of friends from the restaurant where I waitressed. Someone had a pontoon boat, and we were excited to enjoy the sun and water on a rare day off.

My friend anchored the boat, and we began taking turns jumping into the lake. When it was my turn, I jumped off the edge, but my finger caught a piece of metal on the ladder and was cut deeply. It was a freak accident. To this day, I have the jagged mark from that wound's stitches. Every time I am on a boat, I think of that accident.

Like the scar from that accident, the scars of our disappointments are with us for a lifetime. That said, though the scar will be present, the pain will lessen over time and the scar itself may fade as well. Having an understanding of how to manage the painful parts of grief can empower you to heal and grow. These six strategies will help you as you encounter grief's grip on your healing journey.

Strategy #1: Honor Grief in the Little Moments

When I had my first son, I was in labor for thirty-six hours. I had preeclampsia and had to be induced, but I wanted a vaginal delivery. Unfortunately, I was being given two drugs that worked against each other—magnesium and Pitocin. It was a brutal, painful labor. I remember at one point being given some medicine to help with the pain and to give me a little time to breathe and rest.

I recalled this when I heard author and speaker Valarie Kaur give an analogy at a conference. She talked about how when we are in labor, some of the hardest parts are during transition, which is the last stage of labor just before the baby is born. It can feel like we are dying, but it's quite the opposite. Transition is where the new life happens. But to make it through transition, you have to breathe. You have to breathe to be able to push out the new life.

The same is true with grief. Sometimes we have to stop and breathe, allowing all of it to wash over us, before we can get back up and push. Allow yourself the gift of space when you need it. Take the moments you need to breathe so that you can continue to push and experience new life.

I remember that when Matthew first came out and we decided to divorce, my grief—over my marriage ending, losing time with my kids, and having to start over—was a constant sorrow. Everything was blanketed in sadness. I didn't understand how other people could be walking around and seemingly "normal" when my entire life was falling apart. I didn't know how I would get through. Grief is a thief of time, of happiness, of perspective. It makes everything gray.

Now, years later, the sadness pops up much less frequently, and I am no longer walking around in the haze that enveloped me in those early months. What I've learned, though, is that grief can still break through. When this happens, it often points me to something that hasn't yet been acknowledged or fully processed and I need to be openhearted to receive that lesson. If I push it aside, I will only be forced to keep avoiding it. But if I am curious about it, I can learn something about myself or something that I need.

Recently, grief popped up at the most unexpected time. I was on a call with my financial adviser, who is a gentle, smart, and kind man. He has been generous with his time and guidance during this period of transition for me, both personally and professionally. Our calls typically cover a myriad of financial topics, all of which are new territory for me since divorcing.

At the end of the call, I started to get choked up because I realized that since I am no longer married, he is the person I talk to about financial decisions. I was a bit embarrassed as I thanked him for being a safe person for me to ask questions and make decisions with. Not having a spouse means that, for the first time in my life, I don't have a partner to help me with those important decisions. My financial planner was gracious, professional, and kind as I blubbered a bit about this realization and my appreciation for his guidance.

When I ended our Zoom call, I got teary. I missed my old life and hated making so many decisions on my own. So much of my work has been around the big grief of losing a partner, but I had spent less time on the little things. Another divorced friend and I talked about how people who haven't gone through a divorce don't always understand that you don't just mourn the end of the marriage as a whole; you actually mourn the vast individual losses of the past and future.

On that call with my financial planner, the "death" was not having someone to talk to about SEP-IRAs. I jotted a note to myself to talk to my therapist about it. I talked to a friend. And I acknowledged my growth since my divorce, for it is no small thing. I gave myself the space I needed to feel the grief and move through it.

Robin Arzón, vice president of fitness programming and head instructor for Peloton, once said in a class, "Your vulnerability doesn't show what's fractured; it shows what's healing." That call and those tears showed me an area of healing. I was learning new things, becoming more independent and confident, and though I was alone, I was going to be okay.

Honor your grief when it shows up. Make space to feel, to process, and to gain insight. Grief is not something to resent or feel ashamed of.

Strategy #2: Open Up About Your Grief

Sometimes grief is made easier when you tell someone that you are feeling it. Some days I have sat alone in my grief, crying, thinking, praying, and just being with it. When I look back, those were the hardest days because I was experiencing them alone. Now when I'm having a sad day, I will often reach out to a trusted friend or family member and say, "Today I'm feeling sad because of this." Or I'll share an experience that happened and how it made me feel. I remember having a hard day and calling a friend in tears. After we processed for a bit and I was feeling better, I said, "When will I be done crying? I am just so tired of crying."

Simply speaking the truth of how we are feeling relinquishes the power of its hold on you. My friend and I discussed how the reasons why I was crying and feeling emotional were valid. Instead of beating myself up, I gave myself the freedom to feel and work through my grief that day. It is important for us to let go of concerns or fear of judgment and to be willing to let somebody else help hold the sorrow.

I'll never forget the time I went over to my friend Angie's house. Angie is the godmother to my oldest son, has watched my three children be born, and is one of my dearest, oldest friends. We have both been there for each other during the best of times and the worst of times. On this day, I was in the thick of daily grief, and on this particular evening I was especially blue. Very few people knew what I was walking through, but she did.

Angie's kitchen has a seating area with two overstuffed leather chairs. I sat in one chair, and she sat in the other, and as I recounted the day's happenings, I bawled. The path ahead seemed impossible, and the grief was unbearable. She didn't have any tissues, and I remember a brief laugh breaking through my tears as I went through endless wads of toilet paper.

Somewhere in the middle of my story, she crawled into my lap, wrapping her arms around my neck, and just held me as I cried. I remember her small body's weight, physically bringing comfort to mine, her breathing slowing my own. I don't remember specifically what I was crying about that night, but I remember that I was safe, because I wasn't alone in it.

Don't be afraid to invite others into your grief story. I promise, they can help you carry the weight of your pain. Moreover, it will be an honor for them to do so. By talking to someone about your grief, you empower them to help you. Keeping silent doesn't allow your loved ones to know how to help or to be aware of the pain and struggle you are facing. But when you are forthright, they can then act in a way that is caring and helpful.

STRATEGY #3: Respond with Gentleness Toward Yourself

Because grief affects our stories for a long time, it can sometimes be difficult to continue to give ourselves permission to live with it and its ramifications.

On a cold January day, I noticed my thumb reach underneath my fingers to my ring finger, looking for my wedding ring. It had been more than three years since the weight of that platinum band circled my third finger. I didn't realize until I took it off how much I used to play with it, my thumb twisting the ring from side to side, moving it, and being reminded that it signified Matthew's love for me. And now, I still find myself occasionally looking to twist that ring. It's like my body can't remember what my heart knows. I am not married anymore. Matthew doesn't love me as his wife. My thumb will reach and my mind will trick me, asking, *Where is my ring?* And then just as fast, it remembers. It used to be that an action like that would send me into a tailspin of grief and sorrow. And on those days, I gave myself permission to feel all that I was feeling and grieving that day. Because it wasn't just a ring. It was a marriage, a life, and a dream—and it all looked different from what I imagined. Maybe you can relate?

It is possible that you have been living in a cycle of surviving for so long that the idea of being gentle and sitting with your grief feels counter to your expectations. I get it. For a long time, I was so performative in my day-to-day that I became very adept at not allowing my grief to take up much space. But this is not sustainable, and eventually the grief will overflow into everything.

By allowing grief the space it needs and responding with compassion and gentleness toward those feelings, you will move into healing and thriving. It takes work and grace to say, *I am going to show up as my full messy self,* but when you allow that to happen, you will find relief.

The simplest way to go about this is to treat yourself the way you would a friend. If a friend came to you and was down, you wouldn't say, "You shouldn't be sad. Get over it." You would give them a hug, hold space, and be gentle. Offer yourself the gift of that same kind of care. Reframe any negative self-talk to words of kindness toward yourself.

I sometimes find it hard to create space for comfort and gentleness with myself. I tell myself it is lazy or unproductive. If you find yourself thinking similar thoughts, redirect yourself. You are not a machine that needs to constantly produce. You are a human who has a multitude of feelings and emotions, and all of them deserve tending to. On the days that those emotions need more tending, the best thing you can do is acknowledge them and respond with gentleness. You can be productive another day.

On those hard days, I have a list of a few things that I know will help me feel cared for by myself. These include:

- Going for a walk or moving my body in some way.
- Putting on cozy pajamas.
- Eating a comforting meal or ordering takeout.
- Taking a hot bath.
- Going to bed early.

Think about gentle things that you can do for yourself to care for your mind and body on hard days. Focus on those practices and give yourself space to move through those emotions instead of pushing them aside or criticizing them.

Strategy #4: Have a Funeral for the Loss

I talked with my therapist about how the ending of my marriage didn't feel like one big loss. It felt like a battlefield of a thousand deaths. I imagined it like one of those battle scenes from a war movie, where everywhere you looked you saw destruction and loss. I then listed some of the dreams that had died with the ending of my marriage, from big things like growing old with the same person to small things like no longer having a person to go with me to the movies. I mourned it all.

She suggested that I plan a funeral to acknowledge the magnitude of the loss. She thought that ritual might help with my healing, as would naming the things that I lost.

I thought about this suggestion for several weeks. Was it too dramatic? Did I really need a funeral for my marriage? I shared the concept with several friends, and they all encouraged me to do it. I found a date that would work and invited a few close friends to a friend's firepit for an evening of reflection, prayer, and candlelight. As the night grew closer, I became overwhelmed. It just felt like one more thing to do, and it felt like I was creating something that I didn't really want. The night the funeral was to take place, storms were forecasted and I was hit with a migraine.

I canceled the funeral.

One of my friends laughed and said, "How many people get to cancel a funeral?" I laughed as well, but I also felt a twinge of relief.

Though we didn't have that ceremony, I still wrote a eulogy. Much of it was really personal, but the exercise was so helpful for me in reflecting on and honoring the grief over my marriage ending and my relationship with Matthew changing.

I would encourage you to consider writing a eulogy for your own disappointment. Maybe it's the marriage you wanted, the parent you wanted to be, the way you have previously lived, or something else. Frame your disappointment as something you are going to lay to rest but want to honor. Some questions to consider:

- What will you miss about the person/life/thing?
- What special memories do you have?

- What memories had you hoped to create but won't get to?
- What do you want to hold on to from this person/experience?
- What did this person/experience/thing teach you?

Strategy #5: Grow and Show Tenderness

Prior to my divorce, I had compassion for suffering, but no real understanding of it. My life had been easy. The difficult moments weren't *that* difficult. But then, everything changed.

Suddenly, loss, grief, and heartbreak weren't just things I read about in books or saw on Instagram. I had tasted their bitterness. I developed an acute awareness of suffering. The loss of my marriage, of the man I thought I knew, of my time with my children, of the family I had always wanted—it was all coupled with a profound grief.

And that grief created a sensitivity and tenderness for others going through hard times. Suffering doesn't mean our stories end, though when you're in the midst of it, it seems like it is the end. How can anything good come from dust? But as you climb out from the pit, you begin to see how you have been refined by the grief. Suddenly, you find that you see the world and its people differently.

Because of my pain, I am a kinder person. I am more compassionate, gentle, and understanding. I appreciate the difficulty of being human, and I am able to sit with people in a more thoughtful way.

Your experience will allow you to show tenderness to other people in a way that you previously couldn't. It is transformative to be able to say "Me, too" to someone who might not know anyone else walking the path they are on. To come alongside someone in their struggle is a privilege. Grief gives us that understanding and opportunity.

The human experience is nuanced, and the greatest nuances are often formed because of suffering. There's a saying that no one with a good story has an easy life. My story is richer now because of my pain, and I am grateful that I can show more tenderness to others because of my story.

Strategy #6: Trust That Healing Comes

I once had to have an appendectomy. The surgeon went in through a previous surgical scar so that another scar would not be created. That original scar looked a bit rough, and I asked if she would repair it when she sewed me up. She said she would do her best.

That surgical incision took a long time to heal. It kept bleeding and was very painful. The process of healing was slow, and some days I thought the wound would never stop festering. Finally, though, it did. But the scar that I asked to be made better did not heal as I hoped. The scar was actually bigger than before.

When I asked the surgeon why it hadn't healed in the way I hoped, she said, "I did my best, but that type of scar tissue takes a specialist. I am not trained in that way." Her job was to remove my appendix, which she did beautifully. The scar was a result of how my body healed.

The same is true for grief. Healing does come, and things do get better, but it doesn't always look how we want it to. We might wish we could forget, or that things will be as they once were. That is unlikely. But the pain is gone. The healing on the inside still happens. Achieving that inner trust that you will heal takes a bit of confidence, which may feel challenging to find on the hard days. But the work that you are doing to slowly heal does add up. Over time, that work will pay off into healing that will allow you to feel less sad.

Anne Lamott once wrote for the *Washington Post*,[1] "In my younger days, when the news was too awful, I sought meaning in it. Now, not so much. The meaning is that we have come through so much, and we take care of each other and, against all odds, heal, imperfectly. We still dance, but in certain weather, it hurts. (Okay, always.)"

Her wisdom really resonated with me. We heal because we have no choice but to do so. The wounds get smaller, scab over, and scar. And yet, they might affect us when we dance. But the point is, we still dance. I urge you, beloved one, to dance, or work toward dancing again.

My grief has taught me so much. I learned that I am more than my sorrow. I discovered resilience and fortitude that I didn't know was within me. It opened my eyes to others' pain in a way that I was previously blind to. It was a humbling gift that was forged in fire and will serve me all the days of my life.

CHAPTER 5

FORGIVING OTHERS AND YOURSELF

It's a typical Thursday night and my kids are at it again. Inevitably, one of them comes to me crying about another sibling's actions, and in a bit of an exasperated huff, I shout, "Say you're sorry!" After all, don't they know what they need to do?

"Sorry!" The child spews the apology with not an ounce of actual care toward their sibling. My exasperation didn't help the situation, so I take a deep breath and stop what I am doing to try again.

I go to the child and get down on my knees, so I'm at their level, and say, "Let Mama try again. That was not an apology to your sibling. When we apologize, we are working to repair a wound. Like if you fell and cut your knee really badly and then Mama didn't clean it and put a bandage on it, it would get worse because I didn't repair it. If we don't seek repair, the apology isn't helpful for you or the other person. It would be like that cut that Mama didn't take care of—it would get worse. Does that make sense?"

My child nods their head and goes over to offer a sincere apology. The crying sibling accepts, and they hug and go back to playing together.

That scenario is one that has played out in my house over and over again. Learning to apologize is hard, but learning to forgive is maybe harder. But it was easier for my child to forgive because their sibling had apologized sincerely.

The same is true for adults. When someone apologizes and means it, it is usually easier to forgive. But that doesn't always happen. We may be faced with disappointment from another person's transgressions, and they never offer a sincere apology. This may be due to shame, guilt, fear, reluctance, or a blindness to their actions. Sometimes people don't apologize because of what they fear they will lose, whereas others don't apologize because of how they feel it will make them look. For instance, someone might not want to come forward and apologize because they worry that the relationship will end when they apologize. Others might not apologize because they think that apologizing will make them look weak. Whatever the case, we don't always receive the apology that we believe is merited.

When this happens, we are left with two choices: forgive and move forward with forgiveness, or move forward with resentment. Resentment might sometimes feel like an easier choice if you have been really hurt, but I promise, it is not the choice that will bring about the healing and peace that you want and deserve.

WHAT FORGIVENESS ISN'T

You might be familiar with the popular phrase *forgive and forget*. While this is meant to be a positive sentiment to encourage people that it isn't good to hold grudges, the phrase ties forgiveness to forgetting in a way that is not helpful or accurate. This sentiment is just one of the many things that can be misconstrued as forgiveness. In his book *Forgiveness Is a Choice*, Robert D. Enright tells us that:[1]

Forgiveness is not forgetting: Just because you forgive someone, that does not mean you forget what happened. It means that you are extending grace, mercy, and compassion and moving forward.

Forgiveness is not condoning a behavior: When you forgive someone, it does not mean you excuse their behavior. You are not accepting a behavior as okay just because you extend forgiveness.

Forgiveness is not calming down: Sometimes when someone is angry and then they calm down, we think everything is okay and forgiven. Settled emotions are not the same as forgiveness. In fact, calming down and acting like everything is okay without the acts of apology and forgiveness can cause a lot of harm.

I'll add a few other things forgiveness is not:

Forgiveness is not dependent on someone else: We might think we need an apology to forgive, and while that is nice to receive and can make things easier, it is not required. Forgiveness is something we offer exclusively ourselves.

Forgiveness is not tied to justice: Some people believe that a form of justice needs to occur for forgiveness to be granted, but those things are mutually exclusive.

WHY WE FORGIVE

I have these huge holly bushes in my yard. They line one edge of my property, creating a natural privacy fence. One year, I noticed a tangle of vines that was threading through several of the bushes. It was as if a bush was growing within these holly bushes. The vines were choking the holly, preventing it from flourishing. To remove those vines, we had to massively trim back the bushes, pruning so that the choking vines could be removed. Unforgiveness is like those vines, choking our growth. Eventually, if we don't forgive, bitterness can take over in the same way those vines did.

One of the most important steps in healing and rebuilding is the act of forgiveness. We do not forgive for the person who wronged us; we forgive for ourselves. I didn't always understand this. I used to think that we forgave to make someone else feel better, and sometimes it *does* do that, which is awesome and a gift for that person. But true forgiveness is actually for us. Forgiveness gives us freedom—freedom to begin again and to not be weighed down by emotions like anger and hate.

I love what Jeanne Stevens wrote in the book *What's Here Now?* about forgiveness. She said, "Unforgiveness chains you to your pain. Forgiveness reframes your pain."[2] That visual is so powerful to me. Think about your pain as a ball and chain. It would be incredibly difficult to walk with that around your ankle. Imagine the burden, the frustration, the pain of that metal rubbing your ankle raw. That is what unforgiveness is like. It is a chain that connects you to all the pain you have experienced, and the longer you let it be tied to you, the more it will fester and cause additional ache. You must forgive to relieve yourself of current and future pain.

After Matthew came out, people frequently asked me how I forgave him. They thought that because he had hidden his sexual identity from me for so long, I should resent him, or that forgiveness should be really difficult. But honestly, resenting Matthew was not something I spent very long on because the ramifications of resentment were so negative. Resenting Matthew or holding on to unforgiveness would have only hurt me, him, and our kids. Forgiveness allowed me to look ahead and rebuild a new relationship with him. Today we are really close friends and excellent co-parents. We talk multiple times a day. He's often the first person I call when I have news to share—good or bad. If I call and need help, he always says, *Yes, of course, I'm on my way.* One time I called him because a toilet backed up and I couldn't plunge it, and he was over within five minutes. He has been so good to me, and I think that is in large part because of forgiveness.

Of course, in the healing stages, when feelings of resentment crept in, I was quick to explore why with myself and sometimes with my therapist. Forgiveness doesn't have to happen all at once. Like healing, it can be a process.

I have seen the aftermath of unforgiveness, and it is not something that I want for my life. I once knew someone whose ex-husband made some poor choices, leaving her for someone else and in financial ruin. Her situation was awful. But it was made worse because in the years following her divorce, she refused to forgive him, which caused extreme resentment, bitterness, and hate in her life. The poison of that unforgiveness affected her daily life and bled into her extended family and the way they interacted with her ex. It was incredibly toxic and difficult to navigate for all involved. This is what unforgiveness does. It is like cancer, eating away at everything in its path. The only cure for it is to release those feelings and step forward in forgiveness.

OFFERING FORGIVENESS

You might have heard of the Japanese practice of kintsugi, which literally means "gold seams." In this practice, a cracked vessel is repaired with gold. The idea is that the repair of what was once broken makes the thing more beautiful, not less. I think that offering forgiveness is like this practice of adding gold. The crack of what happened and needs repair may remain, but that doesn't mean the situation can't be made more beautiful.

Of course, Matthew apologized to me for keeping his orientation a secret for so long. I was able to offer forgiveness, which made our relationship today possible. We respect each other, care for each other as co-parents and close friends, and still celebrate each other. I can't imagine a life where I did not offer forgiveness to him, because it brought more beauty to my own.

Like my child who was crying at the beginning of this chapter, you, too, might find yourself on the receiving end of an apology.

Aaron Lazare studied more than a thousand apologies, in both public and private contexts. In the book *On Apology*, he provides the following list of qualities of successful apologies, which are successful because they satisfy one or more psychological needs of the offended person or group:[3]

- Restoration of self-respect and dignity
- Assurance that both parties have shared values
- Assurance that the offenses were not their fault
- Assurance of safety in their relationships
- Seeing the offender suffer
- Reparation for the harm caused by the offense
- Having meaningful dialogues with the offenders

If someone has wounded you and apologized, consider this list and what the apology did for you and your relationship. What needs did you have? Did the apology satisfy one of them? Or, if you have not received an apology that you think should be offered, what needs have not been met because you haven't received that apology? I found this list helpful because it offered perspective on why apologies carry so much weight and the release that can happen when we receive one. Forgiveness is transformative for the person who offers it.

I think it is important to acknowledge that just because we forgive, it doesn't mean we forget our woundings or what has happened to us. Our story matters, and to "forget" is to deny our pain. But if we use these memories as points of contention or resentment, then we still have work to do when it comes to forgiveness. True forgiveness is a relinquishing of the bad and its hold on us. And with this forgiveness comes freedom.

It is important to not offer forgiveness until you are ready. For instance, if someone apologizes to you and you say you forgive them but still resent them and hold a grudge, then that forgiveness was not really felt or given. You must be ready to take the step forward of forgiving and letting go before you can say "I forgive you." It is okay to say, "Thank you for those words. I am still processing and need more time." Depending on the transgression or trauma, significant time might be needed for the forgiveness process. Apologies can make a great difference in forgiveness. But sometimes, that forgiveness is still difficult.

WHEN FORGIVENESS IS DIFFICULT

I've heard people say, "If my spouse did X, I would never forgive them." Or, "If X happened to me, I would never forgive that." These types of *never* statements are only hurtful to you. If you find it difficult to forgive someone, ask yourself these questions:

- Why have I not forgiven this person?
- What feelings and emotions could be making it difficult to forgive?
- What do I need to be able to move forward? How can I get what I need?
- Do I need support from someone or a group to be able to release my feelings? If so, how can I get that support?

Forgiveness is often easier for people to grant when their transgressor has asked for forgiveness or tried to repair the relationship or wrongdoing in some way. But sometimes we have to forgive someone who has not asked for forgiveness. In *Forgiveness Is a Choice*, Robert Enright outlines four guideposts for forgiving:

- Phase 1: Uncovering your anger
- Phase 2: Deciding to forgive

- Phase 3: Working on forgiveness
- Phase 4: Discovering and release from emotional prison[4]

Each of these phases requires significant work. Having a trusted therapist work through these phases with you will help bring the healing needed to truly forgive. Regaining control of your story often requires deep work, and forgiveness may be one of the first steps you take.

While it is more difficult to extend forgiveness when you have not received an apology, it should still be pursued. The Mayo Clinic cites the following benefits of forgiveness:[5]

- Healthier relationships
- Improved mental health
- Less anxiety, stress, and hostility
- Fewer symptoms of depression
- Lower blood pressure
- A stronger immune system
- Improved heart health
- Improved self-esteem

I think it's easy to understand that forgiveness can help us from an emotional and spiritual perspective, but I don't think we consider what it does for us physically. Research demonstrates that forgiveness is good for our health in every way. I know that I have felt the positive ramifications in my body many times over the course of my life. You can sometimes actually feel your blood pressure reduce because of an act of forgiveness. It truly is transformative and so good for us.

FORGIVING YOURSELF

Something I really grappled with after my divorce was forgiving myself for not knowing that Matthew was gay. I felt somehow responsible for the fact that we were married for so many years and had three children, and I didn't know that he was gay. How could I not know? This was the person I was closest to in the world. The person I had shared every hope and dream with. The person who knew me maybe better than I knew myself. And yet, I obviously didn't know him in the same way. To admit that, even here, years later, is still hard.

It was made even harder because the most common question I hear from people, usually those who are hearing the story for the first time, is, "Did you know? Did you have even an inkling?" It got to the point where I would start to preemptively say, "My husband came out, but I never knew."

I had to release myself from the *shoulda, woulda, coulda*s and forgive myself. I simply could not have done anything differently. I didn't know because Matthew didn't want me to know. Heck, for a long time, he didn't want to admit it to himself, though that is his story to share. Ultimately, my work had to be to forgive myself for not knowing sooner and blaming myself.

In your story, you might also want to blame yourself, and that blame may cast a cloud of unforgiveness over your life. You might roll through your own set of questions and thoughts for how you got here.

I should have known _____.

I should have realized _____.

I should have done _____.

I should have seen _____.

Remember, hindsight is always 20/20. Letting those thoughts take up space in your mind is only going to slow your process of moving forward. Offer yourself forgiveness and grace for doing the best that you could in your circumstances.

ASK FOR FORGIVENESS

As you work on rebuilding, you might discover areas where you need to ask for forgiveness. If you need to do so, do not ignore this. Admitting fault takes courage and character. When you seek to repair:

- Admit what you did wrong.
- Seek to correct anything that can be corrected.
- Honor space if needed.

Like with healing, you might not be aware of areas where you need to ask for forgiveness right away. But as you uncover parts of your story that you have buried, if you realize forgiveness is needed, by all means seek it out. It is never too late to right a wrong.

You also might find that as you are growing and changing, you sometimes make missteps that require an apology. Or you might find that you are quicker to apologize in a situation as you grow. Recently I had an interaction with a stranger, and I spoke more sharply than I should have. I was overwhelmed about something else, and my frustration about that situation bled into my interaction. I was quick to go back to that person and apologize and explain why I had responded so harshly. She was gracious and accepting and gave me some encouragement, which was really kind of her. I don't think I would have sought out forgiveness at all a few years ago— I simply would have moved on. But now, I want to repair quickly if I am in the wrong. I find that it brings so much more peace and happiness.

SEEK CLOSURE

After my divorce, I started dating (I'll share more in the chapters to come), and I went through a tough breakup. The man ghosted me, and for a long time I never really knew why. He would not get on the phone with me. I finally broke up with him with a video message I texted to his phone because he stopped answering my calls.

For more than a week, I was haunted, trying to understand why. What changed? What went wrong? Why would he not tell me? It was consuming. I cried for days.

A few days after I sent that video message, I had an appointment with my therapist, Stephanie. I told her everything, crying all the way through it. She had sat with me from the earliest parts of my marriage unraveling and is one of the safest people I know. Toward the end of the conversation she said, "You know, you don't have to have all the information to have closure."

I replied, "Hold on, I need to write that down so I can chew on it." I am an information gatherer. I should have gotten a job working for the FBI because I love information. In this case, what was preventing me from moving forward, forgiving him, and letting go was that I wanted to know the why. My therapist said, "You have enough information to know he wasn't right for you. At worst, he lied about who he was; at best, he was truthful; but he still ghosted you. You have all the information you need to end this chapter."

A few days later, we did reconnect. I got the answers that I had been looking for. He hadn't lied, but he had ghosted. There was misunderstanding and hurt on both sides—as is usually the case. Because of my conversation with my therapist, I was mentally in a healthy place to engage with him. We were both tender and kind while still recognizing that we weren't a perfect match. We committed to keeping in touch and remaining friends—and we have and we are.

I have often thought about the idea of not needing all the information to have closure and to forgive. We can so easily become consumed with the whys and the details that we miss the big picture. In my case, the big picture was that, by ghosting me, he had not shown me the emotional connection that I needed. I was able to forgive him for the way the relationship worked out and move forward.

MOVING FORWARD

At the beginning of 2024, I heard Pastor Kevin Queen say during a church service, "We can't build into the new if we're holding on to the past . . . You can't build into a new calling and romanticize the past. We have to let go of what's behind us to press on toward what's ahead. If we want to run our race, we have to look forward, forgetting what's behind and pressing on toward what's ahead."[6]

I think what is important about what Kevin was saying is that we need to release our grip on the past and look forward so that we can really invest in what is ahead. If you have one foot in the past and one foot in the future, you will remain perpetually stuck.

Remember that big snowstorm I mentioned earlier? To understand the implications, you have to understand the city. Typically, Nashville receives about four inches of snow a year, and a snowfall of eight inches in one day will shut the city down for three to five days. And then we got freezing rain three days later.

I live on a hill, which you access from another hill. Driving those hills in those conditions was impossible. The only way to leave our house, for days, was to walk, and that was treacherous. So what did we do? We stayed in, cozy in the comfort of my home. We ate chili and baked brownies. We had nightly fires and played games. It was comfortable and safe.

But eventually, we got stir-crazy. We sensed that others who didn't live on this hill were getting out and doing things. We ran out of milk, bread, cheese, and pizza (all the major food groups). I took a risk and slowly drove my minivan down one hill and then the other. I made it to the grocery store. I've never been so happy to buy dairy in my whole life. While the roads were bad, they weren't impassable. And once I got down those two hills, the roads were actually mostly fine.

This is what life is like. We will often stay in our warm little house on the hill, protecting ourselves from anything bad happening. And at first it is okay. But eventually, we must venture out. And when we do, we learn that what we feared wasn't so bad. Or it was bad (like the ice on my hill), but then it gets better (like the main roads beyond my house).

When it comes to forgiveness, it can also be like those icy roads. It can feel dangerous from the outside, but if you take a step out and forgive (or drive on the roads), you will likely feel as free as I did at the grocery store. Forgiveness is a process, but it is worth venturing out and pursuing.

As you take time to dream about what changes you want to make moving forward, consider the following questions. For me, I looked at things holistically:

- What changes did I want to make to get healthier (physically, mentally, emotionally)?
- What changes did I want to make in my home?
- What values and characteristics did I value in a new partner?
- What did I want to leave behind?
- What was no longer serving me well?
- Was I happy in my parenting? My self-care? My work? If not, what changes needed to be made?

This 360-degree analysis of your life is time-consuming, and you likely won't do it all at once. But don't skip this step. Roses must be pruned to flourish. Will they continue to grow if they are not pruned? Yes. But you won't get the same quantity and quality of flowers and the same healthy plant that you will get if you prune.

The same is true for your life. Now is the time to prune so that you can grow. Apologize. Forgive. Begin to rebuild. Doing so will help you flourish as you rebuild a life you'll love.

CHAPTER 6

REGAINING CONTROL (YES, IT'S ACTUALLY POSSIBLE)

When I was twenty-one years old, I graduated from college, bought my first car (a silver Volkswagen Beetle), moved to Nashville from Wisconsin (where I had been born and raised), and started my first "real" job, all within three weeks. Four months later, I married Matthew. People laughed that I experienced so many big life changes all at once, but to me it was exciting, and I was ready. I was like Joy in the Pixar movie *Inside Out*. Everything was great, all the time. Change was not daunting for me, though for many it would have been.

Sixteen years later, I felt considerably less excited about all the changes I was experiencing. I looked a lot more like the other *Inside Out* characters, especially Sadness. My companions were grief, disappointment, uncertainty, and shame. And how could I not feel those things? As I've shared, I gave myself permission and freedom to move through those feelings. It was so important. But eventually, I turned a corner and I began to again feel the way twenty-one-year-old Jessica felt. Joy emerged, with hope not far behind. I sensed that I was on the precipice of something big, new, different, and exciting. I didn't ask to be here, but here I was.

It's like the time I visited the Smoky Mountains. The drive to get there feels long. An endlessly winding road. And suddenly, you arrive at the spot with a huge lookout where, on a clear day, you can see five states. It's magnificent and vast.

The same is true in life. One minute you can feel like you are traveling an endless, winding road, and the next minute, your world has gotten much bigger and more beautiful. You can see through the fog, and where you thought you might find a few trees, you discover forests of grandeur.

Maybe you, too, can relate to feeling like you are on a precipice of possibility. It feels overwhelming to look out into those mountains. Scary. Unfamiliar. Sometimes foggy. But also, a little exciting. Do you sense that in your soul? The feeling of something new? That goodness might be just beyond what you can see? Don't push it away. Instead, lean in and get ready to soar. Or maybe you are still on that winding road. That's okay, too. You will get there.

In Richard Paul Evans's book *The Four Doors*, he writes, "How we change is in direct correlation to our choices and the power and exercise of our free will."[1] I love that perspective. Our change trajectory is directly due to our own choices. We have the control. Even if we didn't initiate the cause, we still control our reactions and next steps. With that knowledge, let's dive into what it is you want in the wake of your disappointment and how to move forward.

WHAT DO YOU REALLY WANT?

From the time Matthew came out to me until the time he moved out was nine months. The irony of that is not lost on me. You see, I had horrible pregnancies, the types of pregnancies where, when you hear about them, you silently say to yourself, *Please, may that not happen to me.* Almost from the moment I peed on the stick, I was puking. Morning, noon, and night. And that was just the beginning. I had sciatica. I was swollen everywhere. I couldn't sleep. I developed pre-eclampsia twice. When people saw me, they would say things like, *How much longer? You look ready. Is it twins?* (It never was.) I was just big, uncomfortable, and, frankly, miserable. I wanted to be done with the baby-growing-in-my-belly stage.

And then, my babies were born. The labors were hard (two lasted more than twenty-four hours and the third was a C-section). When those babies arrived, I went from being miserable to being overjoyed. The newborn stage is one that starts in a fog, thanks to the sleep deprivation, nursing, and general overwhelm that comes with a new baby. If you have had a baby, you know that the transition after birth is a slow, hard, special time.

This is all strangely similar to the last nine months of my marriage before Matthew moved out. That nine-month period was horrible. I didn't know what to expect or what we were going to do. When one painful thing would end or be solved, something else would come up. Good days never stretched for very long. The tension between us was palpable. I didn't know how life was going to look after he moved out and went public about his sexual orientation. Some days I felt like I wouldn't survive, just like those days when I was throwing up all day during my pregnancies. I felt like I had no control over what was happening to me, just like when I was pregnant and had no control over the misery I felt in my body.

Once we made the decision to divorce, though, I knew I was going to overcome the pain and suffering. It was like I was in the newborn fog, with the worst—those awful pregnancies—behind me. But my path forward wasn't clear. I had to think about what I wanted and the life I was going to make on my own. I had agency that felt new and different because the only person I was now accountable to was me.

Slowly—like when your baby starts sleeping through the night and you start to feel normal again—I began to get clarity. I started to feel myself in my body. I found myself recognizing what I wanted and didn't want, and I started taking action on those things.

I don't know what you are going through or what your disappointment is. But what I do know is that making changes and living differently (whether you chose this path or not) is hard. Making those changes creates forward momentum to move you toward a more whole way of living. Let's take a look at some of the ways you can evaluate and create positive change in your life.

REGAIN CONTROL

Feeling like you have a lack of control when experiencing a disappointment is a normal emotion. After all, you didn't choose:

The cancer diagnosis

The affair

The financial disaster

The job loss

The divorce

The _____

I get it. I didn't have control over my husband coming out. Matthew and I were supposed to be like the old couple in *The Notebook* and die in a nursing home, holding each other. I thought it would be better than the pain of our marriage ending and being faced with such a big truth. But that doesn't mean my disappointment had to ruin my entire life or get the best of me. I was fortunate to have many things that I could control in my life.

My attitude

My healing

My growth

My relationships

My next steps

Each day was a bit of "fake it till you make it," because I certainly didn't want this story, but there was no way in hell I was going to let it get the best of me. While I didn't have control of what happened with Matthew coming out, I did have control of my story moving forward. It was a season of reclaiming myself and my needs in a way I never had as an adult. I was like Kelly Clarkson singing,

> What doesn't kill you makes you stronger
> Stand a little taller
> Doesn't mean I'm lonely when I'm alone

I spent a lot of time thinking about what I wanted, the changes I wanted to make in my life, and how I was going to overcome my sorrow. In truth, some of the things I wanted were things I wanted during my marriage, but either the timing didn't make sense or I hadn't given myself permission to vulnerably share those desires. They were not new longings, but my divorce was the first time I made space to acknowledge and pursue them. Some of these included taking the leap to pivot in my career (something Matthew and I had talked a lot about, but we always found a reason to wait) and pulling the trigger on some big home renovations. I also regretted that I didn't communicate better in certain areas of our relationship, and I knew I wanted to improve in that aspect with future partners. Other changes I wanted to make were totally new, given my new circumstances. For instance, I thought about what I wanted in a partner, how I wanted to manage finances differently, and what I wanted my work/life balance to look like. Basically, I took my divorce as an opportunity to begin again, and everything was on the table.

The season you are in or have been in might be challenging, like my pregnancies. You might still be in that season, or you might be in the newborn fog. Either way, it is important to recognize that you might have longings that you have not acknowledged. This might be the first time you admit that there is something you want or need. That may feel uncomfortable, but I want to encourage you to do it anyway. Disappointment can often be a catalyst for change, if we are willing to make the space and do the work of changing. And those changes mean you taking control of your story and your next steps.

The effort of the work is what sets you up for success. A year ago, I developed Achilles tendonitis in both of my feet. You don't realize how helpful your Achilles tendons are until they are constantly in pain. My pain would flare up and die down, but I didn't make an appointment to see an orthopedic doctor for months. When I finally went in, he requested X-rays. He then examined those and my feet and said yep, you need to start physical therapy. But then I didn't make the appointment right away. Some personal things were going on, and I just didn't take that next step forward for several months. When I finally saw the physical therapist, he said the Achilles tendonitis was pretty bad and it would likely take a year of doing exercises to bring about healing. But he assured me that I would heal.

This was in November. I was sporadic at best with doing the exercises, and I didn't feel like they were really bringing me relief. So three months later, I decided I needed to find a physical therapist closer to my house so that I could go for consistent appointments and really take care of this issue. When I met my new physical therapist, I was blown away by how different he was from my previous provider. His bedside manner was caring, he was clearly knowledgeable, and he really listened to me. I started going to see him twice a week. At each appointment, I would look around the room at all the other people doing exercises to become well. What I noticed is that everyone's work was small. Meaning, no one was running fast. No one was doing quick reps. Everything was methodical. Concentrated. Small. My movements included toe raises. Small ankle movements with a band. It was hard to believe that these movements were going to make me better. But they were. And they did.

The same is true when it comes to moving forward after disappointment. You are likely not going to make a bunch of massive changes all at once. Instead, you will slowly invest in one thing at a time. One action. One choice. One day at a time. And then suddenly, you will be somewhere different. You will be better than before. You will be changed. And all those small, methodical movements that didn't seem like much in the moment add up to healing and wholeness.

The unexpected happens in life. It is the beauty and the pain of life. But just because we experience things outside our control, it doesn't mean that we don't have any control at all. We do. You can make choices to do something new, different, and unfamiliar. You can take steps you never thought you could or would because you didn't need to. Now you must. Maybe it is by choice or maybe it is because you feel like you have no other option. Either way, put your shoes on and step forward.

You are on the brink of something new. What you are currently living is not what you want, or you wouldn't be reading this book. You get to take the reins back on your life and create a life you love. In the book *The Top Five Regrets of the Dying*, by Bronnie Ware, one of the regrets is, "I wish I had the courage to live a life true to myself, not the life others expected of me."[2] The work you are doing now is courageous and is ensuring that when you die, you do not have that regret. This is not easy work, but it is worth it. I have some exercises that I think will help you to articulate the dreams you have for your life.

EXERCISE 1:
CREATE A "WHAT I WANT"
CIRCLE CHART

Let's make a circle chart to articulate what you really want in life. Draw a circle in the middle of a piece of paper with your name on it, and then, like spokes on a wheel, draw lines with other circles that name the areas and responsibilities in your life, such as work, home, and kids. On those circles, draw lines out with words describing what you want for those things.

For this exercise to be effective, don't hold back. Write down everything on your mind and in your heart. Nothing is too big or too dumb. The point is to dream big and have an imagination for what your life could be. This simple exercise is a meaningful way to codify what you want and your goals for the future.

EXERCISE 2:
A VISION BOARD FOR THE FUTURE

Now we are going to take inspiration from our goals to create a vision board. Get a piece of poster board, scissors, a glue stick, and a bunch of magazines and create a vision board. Think fourth-grade art collage, but for your life. What are images and words that reflect the life you want? Look for those in the pages of the magazines and cut them out, then glue them on the board. Consider:

- What words describe the life you want to have?
- What words describe you?
- What images reflect the life you yearn for?
- What images look like the dreams of your heart?
- What feels daunting and impossible, but you want to make it a reality?

I know it sounds trite, but the only things that are impossible are the things we never ask for and go for. For instance, in my twenties I worked at a PR firm and started a blog. I loved blogging, and I remember a colleague saying to me, "Do you think you could ever do your blog full time?" I scoffed and said, "No way. No one can actually make money doing that and live." For a long time I believed that, but then I started to dream bigger. Now I am doing that very thing. (I'll tell you more about how I got there in a few pages.)

Spend a couple of hours cutting, gluing, and dreaming about the future. I am usually surprised by the way a project like this helps me codify what I want. This vision board will become a visual reminder for you to cling to when you are moving forward in the months to come.

EXERCISE 3:
ARTICULATE YOUR VALUES

As you consider your goals and vision for the future, it is also helpful to think about what you value. Our values are the core tenets by which we live. These are the things we hold precious above all else. When I began dating, I thought a lot about my values and the values I wanted to share with a partner. I knew that some of my values were deeply important and must be shared, while others were not as critical to match up exactly. For instance, I am someone who values family, honesty, and travel. It would not work for me to be with a partner who hated kids, was sneaky, and preferred to stay home.

Knowing your values as they relate to the ways you live, love, and see the world can help to bring focus to your life and the things you want to pursue. For this exercise, I would like you to take the time to write down five to ten values that you hold close, then narrow them down to two or three. Consider what you value around relationships, work, and so on. These values serve as guides for your life and future decision-making. Having clarity around your values will give you wisdom as you navigate new paths.

Here are some values to get you started. For a larger list, check out Brené Brown's free printable for her book *Dare to Lead*.[3] You can also simply add your own words, too.

- Acceptance
- Accountability
- Achievement
- Bravery
- Commitment
- Compassion
- Courage
- Creativity
- Discipline
- Faith
- Family
- Financial stability
- Fun
- Independence
- Kindness
- Loyalty
- Openness
- Respect
- Security
- Time
- Travel
- Vulnerability

My top values

1. _____
2. _____
3. _____
4. _____
5. _____
6. _____
7. _____
8. _____
9. _____
10. _____

Circle your top 2–3 values.

These exercises are worthwhile and significant because you are likely writing things that you have been afraid to say or do. You are boldly reclaiming your life and creating an action plan for your life. Change is coming. Do you sense it?

You get to have a life that you want. The disappointment you have faced or are facing is not the whole story. Let it refine you, not define you. It is not too late.

MANIFESTING

I firmly believe that what we put out into the world matters and that manifesting can be a helpful practice. Think about the most positive people you know. What are they like? What kinds of words do they use? Now contrast that with people who are negative. What are they like? What kinds of words do they use?

The language we speak over our lives matters. I want you to consider starting a practice of manifesting good things for your life. Many resources on manifesting are available if you want to really dive into this practice. (I really loved the book *The Universe Has Your Back* by Gabrielle Bernstein on this subject.) On a basic level, manifesting is speaking out loud the things we want for our life and bringing positive energy for those things to happen. I realize for some this might sound a bit woo-woo, but I have found it to be one of many helpful practices on my healing journey.

Our energy can be used to raise us up or bring us down. By being a force of positive energy in our own lives, we can help create a life we want. We aren't being passive about what has happened to us or how we got to a place that we didn't want. Instead, we take an active role of speaking positivity, light, and hope into our story.

Masaru Emoto, through a series of experiments, discovered that water (yes, water) responds to human words, intentions, and music.[4] If you look him up, you will find images of water crystals that were formed after certain phrases like *I love you* and *I will kill you* were spoken over the water. I know it sounds crazy, but the water literally looked different. Positive phrases created beautiful crystals, and negative phrases created jumbled clumps of mess. The differences were astonishing.

Our bodies are made of water. Think about what this means for you. How can you encourage the very molecules of your body to be more beautiful? Reading about this study caused such a shift for me and the way I thought about words affecting me. It isn't just about shifting our perspective; it is about changing ourselves at a cellular level—literally.

SOW GOOD THINGS

One weekend, while I was visiting my sister's Lutheran church in Wisconsin, the pastor talked about the verse in Galatians that teaches that we will reap what we sow. He started with a mini-lesson for the kids in the congregation and held up a tiny seed. He asked the kids, "What will happen when I plant this seed? What will it need to grow?" "Water!" one child shouted. "Sunlight!" another added. Then the pastor added, "What about time?"

Ah, yes! The kids nodded, and I nodded along with them. Time is the most important factor. Because growth of all kinds requires time.

As you start on this path of reimagining and redefining your life after disappointment, think of your life like a sunflower seed you are planting. Sunflower seeds are kind of ugly, but think of what comes from them: strong, glorious, golden sunflowers that stand tall in the light. Your situation might feel dark and ugly, like that seed. But plant that seed and begin to imagine the future. Sow into it.

For that sunflower of your life to grow, you must sow good things for a long time. You will need to water and nourish that seed. It might be tempting to think our small habits don't matter, but they do. They stack on top of each other and add up to something substantial: positive growth. The seed of your new chapter will need time to emerge from its shell, first underground, where it will establish some roots. Then it will burst from the dirt, first small, then growing tall in the light. It will get strong, hardy, and beautiful.

Can you see it? Can you imagine your life as a beautiful sunflower? And embrace what it will take to grow it from the seed you are now? When we plant things from a seed, it can feel like it takes forever for the plant to grow. Likewise, this might feel true in your life. But it is worth continuing to sow this seed of opportunity in your life, because eventually your life is going to flourish.

BECOME A STUDENT

One of the universal truths of disappointment is that we all experience disappointment because of unmet expectations. Regardless of whether these expectations were valid, understanding the why behind our expectations is important. Ask yourself:

- Why did I believe _____ would _____?
- Who taught me I should believe _____?
- What have I not learned about _____ that will help me in the future?

These are not questions to make you feel judgmental of yourself or your circumstances. Instead they are to prompt curiosity about your story and spur you on to become a student of your situation and what you can learn.

For instance, in my situation, I would answer the questions in the following ways:

Why did I believe my marriage would last forever? I grew up in a Catholic home and saw very few divorces in my family and my family's circle of friends. I was witness to crummy marriages, but even crummy marriages didn't end in divorce. I was a "good girl" and found a "good guy," so I thought divorce wouldn't happen because we were good people. I also believed Matthew when he promised forever when we were married. It was impossible for me to imagine anything else.

Who taught me I should believe that marriage was forever? My parents, family, friends, church, and the media all informed me in my understanding that being married to one person forever is the ultimate goal. As part of this, I also learned that divorce was a failure, even if it was not primarily my fault that my marriage ended.

What have I not learned about marriage and relationships that will help me in the future? I was married at twenty-two and had very few serious relationships before that. My parents were loving parents, but as a couple they did not always model healthy relationship patterns. I was essentially writing a new playbook with few good resources. Some things that I didn't learn were why therapy matters, anything about sex beyond "do it when you're married," how to apologize well, how to deal with disappointment, and how to manage finances.

Whatever the answers are to your questions, let them direct you to the ways you need to become a student. It is never too late to learn. We sometimes think that because we are adults, we "should know this," but instead approach this season with curiosity and permission to say to yourself, "I guess I haven't learned that yet," as Shauna Niequist reminds readers in her book of the same name.[5]

After my divorce, I dove into a lot of books about sex and relationships because I knew I wanted to do things differently and better when I sought out new dating relationships. I learned so much about myself and ways to approach relationships in healthier ways. I also became a student of relationships with the men that I dated. Because I had not dated a lot and ended up marrying a man who was gay, I had many new experiences dating heterosexual men. Every relationship had aha moments for me and caused me to have a lot of growth.

I also started to learn more about ways to manage my finances, because I saw that as another area that could use improvement in my life. I began following financial experts online, reading books, and hiring a financial planner. I was empowered to make decisions that were different from those we made in our marriage because of the learning I was experiencing.

Do not be ashamed of what you don't know. Instead, approach your life with curiosity about what you have to learn, and use that as motivation to work and learn. It is a worthwhile investment to read books, take classes, and talk with experts. The time and energy you spend will change your life for the better.

Remember, you are the director of your life. A director is responsible for looking at the big picture and seeing what is and isn't working. Likewise, when you are faced with what isn't working, it is your responsibility to not stay there. Instead, commit to learning and growing so you can do and be better.

DREAM AGAIN

For years, Matthew and I had talked about me leaving my day job so I could pursue being an influencer full time. But it never seemed like the right time. We never had enough money in savings. A health need would come up, and it seemed like losing my insurance wasn't worth the risk. I am naturally a risk-averse person, and it felt scary. Matthew and I were comfortable with the status quo in a lot of ways in our marriage, and my job was one of those things.

Then Matthew came out, and I was faced with making decisions about everything regarding my life. I was starting over at thirty-eight. Immediately I started thinking about whether it was feasible for me to leave my corporate job.

I remember talking with my friend Angie about my desire to leave my corporate job to become a full-time influencer. I'll never forget when she gently but firmly said to me, "The dream of your marriage died. But this one isn't going to die."

She was right. I did not have control over my marriage ending. The dream of a marriage that lasted a lifetime died a painful death despite all my fighting for it. But the death of my dream job? If that happened, it would be on me. And I was not going to let it happen. I was in control of what I did next.

I started hustling harder in the fringe hours of my workday. Mornings, lunch breaks, evenings—if I found a bit of time, I was working to set myself up for success as a self-employed influencer. I networked more. A friend made an introduction to a business that offered me more partnerships. I saved money.

On an ordinary April day, I gave notice at Vanderbilt Health, where I had worked in the marketing department for a decade. I was so nervous, excited, hopeful, and sad. My colleagues had become more like family than coworkers, and the thought of leaving them made me weep. I knew that my departure would leave a hole in the team, and I felt guilty about the extra work I knew everyone would have to pick up. But I also knew that it was time and that I had to make the change.

Looking back, leaving Vanderbilt Health to become a full-time entrepreneur was the single best decision I made for myself after my divorce. It gave me the agency to redesign a huge part of my life. I now had the flexibility I needed for my children and was able to scale my income in a way that I wasn't able to do working in corporate America. More than all of those things, it gave me the courage for the other changes I was facing.

You deserve to dream. But more than that, you deserve to pursue that dream. Grief is a thief and can make it feel like we don't have permission to dream again, but that couldn't be further from the truth. You do get to dream. And whatever your disappointment, it is not the end.

In the following chapters, we are going to look at some practices that will help empower you as you move forward with the next part of your story.

CHAPTER 7

INVESTING IN FRIENDSHIP

One night I was scrolling Instagram when I saw a friend's post about a getaway trip she had gone on with her husband of over twenty years. In the caption she reflected on a quote that marriage gives us a witness to our lives. The post accompanied a smiling photo of her, with her husband kissing the top of her head. It was meant to be a light and loving post, but when I read it, I started to cry.

I think not having that kind of witness to my life has been one of the hardest parts of divorce. Yes, Matthew is still a close friend, which has been an incredible gift. In many good times and hard times since our divorce, I have called on and depended on him. He has likewise called on and depended on me. But yet, things are different. Of course they are. We aren't married partners. Because I was married so young and for so long, navigating adulthood alone for the first time has been empowering at times and excruciating at other times. It was during this season that I came to really appreciate my circle of friends in a deeper way.

We were made for witness in our lives, and married or not, community is incredibly important. As I have rebuilt my life, I have come to have a deeper appreciation for the friends I have and have been more intentional in creating community in my everyday life. What do I mean by that? How can someone actually do that? How do we walk the path of rebuilding a life we love in community? In this chapter, I am going to talk about navigating the pitfalls that prevent community as well as how to seek friends out and let them in.

NAVIGATING LONELINESS

I have never felt lonelier than in those first months after my marriage ended. If I'm really honest, it is the emotion I struggled with the most. I missed having a partner and the intimacy of someone knowing me and about the goings-on of my life. I've learned that loneliness is a struggle for many people, but it is one we don't talk about enough. Moreover, when we feel lonely, it can overwhelm our ability to reach out to friends, invest in community, or make new friends, though outreach would be the antidote to at least some of those lonely feelings.

Loneliness is so common that in 2023, the surgeon general released a report saying that the United States had a loneliness epidemic.[1] The report stated that one in two adults experience loneliness. It also stated:

> The lack of social connection poses a significant risk for individual health and longevity. Loneliness and social isolation increase the risk for premature death by 26% and 29% respectively. More broadly, lacking social connection can increase the risk for premature death as much as smoking up to 15 cigarettes a day. In addition, poor or insufficient social connection is associated with increased risk of disease, including a 29% increased risk of heart disease and a 32% increased risk

of stroke. Furthermore, it is associated with increased risk for anxiety, depression, and dementia. Additionally, the lack of social connection may increase susceptibility to viruses and respiratory illness.

In an NPR interview about this study, Surgeon General Dr. Vivek Murthy said, "And you can feel lonely even if you have a lot of people around you, because loneliness is about the quality of your connections."[2]

I think disappointment is a breeding ground for loneliness. We close off because we don't want to be a burden, we don't want to seem like we don't have it together (newsflash: no one does), or it feels too emotionally draining to be with someone. Yet, we need community. Loved ones, friends, and even strangers at the library or at church can give us points of connection that help to get us through.

BUSYNESS

Another reason why we don't make time for friendship is because we are busy. In a poll I did on Instagram, I asked my community what prevents them from getting together with friends and received hundreds of comments like:

- Work/life balance, sticking to plans with lots of their kids in the mix, someone gets sick.
- Week is filled with work and sports/activities so don't feel like I get quality time with kids during the week.
- The pressure for things to look a certain way: home, makeup, kids.
- Family and work obligations.
- Exhausted from work.

- My work/life balance is awful. Also, my mom is getting older, I find I'm giving my energy on days off to her.
- Gone for work 12–13 hours a day. Exhausted at night. Chores and errands on weekends.

I could relate to many of the items on this list, and I bet you could, too. This busyness makes it difficult for us to make time for or prioritize friendship. We have so much on our plates that the very thought of adding more to it, even if it is something good like friends, is daunting. Moreover, a lot of the activities making us busy are also important, like work and family obligations, so it can feel challenging to add in friendship.

I started dating a man, and as we were getting to know each other, I would often share about how during the day I had talked to various friends. After a couple weeks, he said, "How do you have time to talk to so many people? You are so busy, but I hear about your friends all the time." I realized that I had built my schedule to include time for relationships. I would talk with my best friend on FaceTime while I did my makeup in the morning, or I would call another friend while eating lunch in the middle of the day.

I like to say, "Five minutes is better than no minutes," meaning that even if I get just a few minutes with them, it is better than not having spent any time chatting. I've also learned that these small bits of time add up. It's like investing. Even if you do just a tiny bit, over time, your money can grow into something substantial. Likewise, small bits of time investing in friendship can lead to rich relationships that will make your life better.

When my marriage fell apart, I am grateful that busyness had not prevented me from investing in friendships, because I really needed my friends. They showed up, as I have written about, in so many ways. Your life is a reflection of what you value. Don't let busyness be a bigger value than friendship.

MINDLESSNESS

Another reason why we might not make time for community is that we are wasting time on mindless activities. This can be particularly evident during times of grief. It can feel easier to not go out with friends, reach out to someone, or invite people over than to do it. Instead, we squander our time binging hours of Netflix or scrolling mindlessly on social media.

I remember when Matthew first moved out, I watched a lot more television than is usual for me. And it wasn't even quality television. It was reality shows and sitcoms—anything that would distract my mind from my heartache.

I also remember it taking more effort to be social. I wanted to just work and be alone. I didn't want to put forth more effort than I had to. And while this is understandable, it doesn't mean it was good for me. Staying at home and engaging in mindless activities was not helpful for my emotional wellness.

But every time I was with people, I felt better. Of course I did. But sometimes we don't have clarity that being with others will be more lifegiving than anything a screen has to offer.

I strongly believe that we make time for what is important to us. No one gets to the end of their life and is like, "Man, I am so happy that I averaged eight hours a day staring at a screen." Consider the ways in which you might be engaging in mindless activities, like scrolling and binging, as a way to numb pain or avoid being with people. You are in control of how you spend your time. Don't waste your time on things that won't have a lasting positive impact.

WAYS TO FIND COMMUNITY

I live on a small cul-de-sac. It is made up of five houses. About seven years ago, a family moved in next door to us who had a boy and a girl about the same ages as my oldest two kids. The four of them became best buddies. We also became friends with their parents, Andrew and Amber. Our kids were always at each other's houses and romping through our yards. We also got along with our other neighbors, but we recognized it would be nice to get to know them better.

One afternoon I sent a text to everyone asking if they would be interested in doing a monthly potluck. I thought we could rotate houses and it would be a fun way for us to get to know each other better. The potlucks went on for about eighteen months, until Andrew and Amber moved away. Their move was timed with the start of the pandemic (and when Matthew and I were talking about separating), and unfortunately we never picked the potlucks back up. But I think about that season often, and how nice it was to share meals and get to know one another better.

All it took for those dinners to happen was a text. You likely have opportunities for community all around you, but it can take some effort to send the text, email an invitation, or coordinate a dinner reservation. If you are someone who has limited community or you are looking to expand or deepen friendships, here are some practical ways you can meet people, grow friendships, and foster community in your own life:

- Connect with your neighbors.
- Join a group at the library or local community center.
- Get involved at your children's school.
- Become a part of a church community group.
- Reach out to people you know on Facebook or post an open invitation in a Facebook group.
- Host something at your home and invite people in your community.

It can feel scary and vulnerable to put yourself out there and seek out community. I recently was in my neighborhood Facebook group and saw a post from a woman who said that she had lived in the neighborhood for several years but knew few people. She said she had a young child and wondered if anyone would want to get together for a playdate. Multiple women responded enthusiastically. I think so often people are yearning for community, but they aren't brave enough to say it aloud. But when they do, magic happens. Like my neighborhood potlucks.

I'll never forget when my friend Shauna Niequist spoke at a conference about inviting people over. She said something like, "The floor just has to be neat enough that people won't trip. Walk around with a laundry basket and just toss everything in it." I loved her brutal honesty and the permission she gave the audience to stop worrying so much about the condition of their homes. Doing so stifles the community we so desperately long for. People never remember the condition of your home; they remember the warmth of how you made them feel when they were there.

Reading those statistics from the surgeon general affirmed my belief that we all want to be invited. We all want to feel seen and known. We are made for community, but the way we live doesn't always make it easy.

THE SEVEN PILLARS OF FRIENDSHIP

As you are rising and rebuilding, it is imperative that you create and cultivate community in your own life. In the book *Friends*, Robin Dunbar outlines the seven pillars of friendship, which are the criteria we use in seeking out friends.[3] These pillars are:

- Having the same language or dialect
- Growing up in the same location
- Having the same educational and career experiences
- Having the same hobbies and interests

- Having the same worldview (an amalgam of moral views, religious views, and political views)
- Having the same sense of humor
- Having the same musical tastes

Since going out on my own as a full-time influencer, I have specifically sought out friends in the same line of work as me. One of the deepest friendships I have grown over the past four years has been my friend Janssen. She and I first became acquainted through some Instagram direct messages. I immediately took a liking to her and asked if she would consider reviewing a course I was building. That project led to both of us talking about work more and building trust with each other. We started FaceTiming and texting, at first weekly, then a few times a week, then nearly every day. We went to conferences and shared business contacts. We talked about intimate details about our business, like money and contracts. I called her crying when boyfriends broke up with me. She became not just a friend, but a best friend. The kind of friend that I hope will stand beside me in a wedding someday.

As I looked at that list of friendship pillars, I realized that Janssen and I have so much in common. It is clear to me that we knock it out of the park on the pillars. That said, even with those commonalities, our friendship took effort from both of us. It took time. It took saying yes to phone calls. It took being vulnerable. And most of all it took love for each other. Janssen has truly become a saving grace for me. When I think about building a life I love, my business is a part of it, and I feel like Janssen's friendship is one of the reasons why I have been able to grow and dream. Her spurring of me and my spurring of her have made both of us better.

I don't know if you have a Janssen already or if you would like to have a friend like Janssen. In either situation, I want to encourage you to put in the effort, because as you rebuild, friendship really matters. No one builds anything substantial alone. You must have friends in your life to help encourage, love, and see you.

SAY YES TO INVITATIONS

Valentine's Day was coming up. I was dreading it. The kids were going to be at their dad's. I was going to be alone. I love holidays, and it just felt sad. And then I got a text from my friend Courtney asking, "Do you have plans for Valentine's Day? If not, do you want to be together? I don't want you to be alone, and I thought it would be fun to be together."

I said yes. I don't remember what we ate or did, but what I do remember is how it made me feel to be thought of on a day that could have been really hard. It was less hard because my friend reached out and gave me plans when I otherwise would have been alone.

Her invitation was also meaningful because I was out of the immediate post-divorce season when people regularly were checking in on me. There is a period of time after a major life change when a lot of people are reaching out and taking time to think of you, but eventually that fades. My divorce had been a few years before, and it was *out of sight, out of mind* for most people. The fact that she remembered was so thoughtful.

Whenever you are invited to something, say yes (if possible). Even if you don't feel like it. Even if you have to hire a babysitter. Even if it is far away. Say yes. I found that saying yes, even when it felt hard emotionally to do so, gave me something to look forward to and provided companionship during my loneliest seasons.

I also think that so often we mistakenly choose the comfortable, familiar, or easy thing, thinking that is the best choice for us. Usually that comes at a cost of saying yes. For instance, it might feel easier to come home after work and watch a reality show versus going out to dinner with friends. But what likely happens if you go out with friends is that they fill your cup in a way that television never will. We have to be brave enough and strong enough to break out of complacency. Don't stay stuck in a rhythm that is not life-giving.

Women have said to me over the years that they feel bad for saying yes to invitations with their friends because it will mean time away from their children. When I look back on my childhood, I remember my mom going out with her friends and don't recall ever feeling sad about that. In fact, I remember being happy when she went out, because we got time with my dad or a fun babysitter, and we noticed that my mom was happy that she spent time with her friends. Pouring into friendship is filling your cup, and a full cup is one that can be poured from. Your kids will be better off because you said yes to invitations and opportunities.

Also, try to be someone who invites other people to your home, to meals, or to other experiences. I have some friends whom I always invite to events, but they never come. I've been tempted to stop inviting them. But then I remember that I once had a friend decline an invitation and she said, "But please keep inviting me." It always feels nice to be invited, so I keep inviting, even in spite of receiving those declines.

WHEN DO YOU SEE FRIENDS?

In considering your friendships, a good place to begin is thinking about when you typically see your friends now (and if this is a rare occurrence, keep reading). I surveyed my Instagram audience to learn about their friendship habits, and I got hundreds of responses. The common themes were:

- At work
- Going out (coffee, lunch, dinner, entertainment)
- At other events (for example, kids' sports)
- The gym
- Gatherings at homes

While at first glance it seemed like people were seeing their friends in lots of ways, most of the gatherings required planning, intentionality, and consistency. For instance, you wouldn't see your friends at church if you skipped on Sunday. And going out always requires someone to ask, make a plan, and then follow through. Basically, friendship takes effort.

There are lots of different types of friends. You might have your work friends, your neighbor friends, your old friends, your kids' friends' parents friends, and social media friends. You might have a few people that fall in the "best friend" category, too. Each of these relationships is valuable, and they all have different weights and roles in your life.

As you evaluate the friends you have, be careful not to get caught up in comparing your friendships with other people's friendships. For instance, a group of friends of mine from college often takes trips together. Old high school friends of mine have been friends for more than twenty-five years. They live in the same town and their kids go to the high school that we once attended. It would be easy to compare these to my friendships with people who haven't been around as long, or to think about how I don't have old friends I travel with year after year. But I have many wonderful friendships. Just because they are different doesn't make them less special and sacred. Your friendships don't need to look like other people's. They simply need to be what you need in your life.

When I worked in an office, a colleague and I both loved to read. We decided it would be fun to start an office book club. Every other month, we would meet at someone's house and discuss a book. The group started with about a dozen of us in 2017, and, astonishingly, it still meets today, having grown to close to thirty members, with fifteen to twenty women gathering each time. I think there are several reasons why the book club has remained intact:

- People long for community. And now, with so many of us working remotely, the book club is a consistent way to see people in person.
- We read great books. Truly, reading great books definitely makes you want to stay in the club.
- It's consistent. Every other month for eight years is a long time. I think we have canceled only a handful of times in all those years. Being dependable matters.
- It is out of our normal element. The group is made up of colleagues and former colleagues in health care. We gather in one another's homes and get to see sides of each other we wouldn't get to see otherwise.
- The leaders make an effort. I, along with my friends Katie and Linda, work to make sure emails get sent out, calendar invites are set, and the group stays together. Our effort inspires the effort of others.

The book club has taught me that it is beneficial to have consistent community built into your life. When I hosted our Christmas gathering, I spoke briefly to the group of women, thanking them for coming that night and for being one of the most consistent groups of women in my life. I got choked up thinking about how that group had been such a constant for me. Having consistent community is especially helpful when you are going through a difficult season. This consistency ensures that you are not alone, that you have something to look forward to, and that you have fun. Book club might not be your thing, and that is okay. It might be a church group, the gym, parents on the sidelines of your kids' sporting events, or some other gathering. If you don't have a group like this, find one. It will bring value to your life.

THE REALLYS IN YOUR LIFE

My daughter is in seventh grade, and I love listening to her tell stories about her friends. They talk all the time, plan sleepovers, and want to spend time together constantly. We went to the beach for spring break, and the part on her scalp got sunburned and started to peel just as she went back to school. I picked her up after school the first day back, and she said, "Mama, my scalp is peeling so bad!" I said, "Yeah, mine is a little, too." She went on to say, "My friends were reallys and helped get the peeling out of my hair."

"Reallys?" I replied. What was she talking about?

"Yeah, reallys. Like they are really my friends because they were willing to do that."

I loved that term and it made me think a lot about who the reallys in my life are. Who are the people who would do anything for me? I am thankful that I have more than a few people who would drop everything to be there for me if I called at a moment's notice. Likewise, I know that I would be on other people's lists in the same way.

I'll never forget when I called my friend Colleen to tell her that Matthew and I were divorcing. We went to college together and she lives in Baton Rouge with her husband and three beautiful daughters. We don't see each other often, but every time we talk, it is like we just picked up where we left off. I knew that the call was going to be hard and shocking when I shared why we were divorcing, but her response was so loving. I'll never forget when she said, "Tell me what you need. I will get in the car and start driving right now if you need me there." Colleen is a really in every way.

Make a list of the reallys in your life.

1. _____

2. _____

3. _____

4. _____

5. _____

Now consider whether you have invited them into your story. Are these the people you went to when we discussed truth-telling in the beginning of this book? If so, how can you keep them involved in your story as you move from disappointment to rebuilding?

HOW PEOPLE MIGHT SHOW UP

If you have told people what you are going through, you might find that they want to show up for you in some way. I asked my Instagram community how people have helped them during a tough time, and here are some of their answers:

- Texted to check on me, brought food over, watched my kids.
- Made me food. It sounds simple but it really was helpful.
- Listening, random encouraging texts, asking questions (including tough ones).
- Calls, texts, visits, sending small gifts/cards.

- Making me laugh. Encouraging notes or texts. Going out of their way to see me.
- Text messages, prayers, showing up, laughs, jumping right in to help.
- Wine drop-offs, supportive texts, shielding from other related situations.

What I loved about these examples is that you can see how these friends took action. They showed up, often without a lot of guidance or prompting. I have learned through my own hard seasons that people want to help. They mean well. That said, sometimes they don't show up like we need.

Once in a while, we need to be brave enough to say we need help and reach out to someone or a friend group. For instance, before I had a big surgery, I asked a friend if she would be willing to set up a meal train for me because I knew that would be a practical way to help our family during my recovery. She was happy to do it, and so many friends delivered meals during that period of time.

In contrast, I once had a friend post on social media a month after she had a baby that it was one of the scariest months of her life because the depression she had battled her whole life came in with a vengeance when she had her baby. I wished I would have known. I would have come over, brought meals, done laundry for her—anything that she needed. I didn't know she was dealing with anything difficult, and so I didn't ask.

When things are hard, people might say to you, "Let me know if you need anything." This is a nice thing to hear, but when you are in the thick of it, you don't even know what to say you need. If that feels familiar, make a list of ways you could use support. You might make a grid with different areas like personal, home, kids, work, and so on. If you can articulate your needs, you then become empowered to speak them aloud.

HUG LONGER

Have you ever heard about the rules around hugging at Disney? Cast members are instructed that when someone hugs them, they should never be the first one to let go from the hug, because you never know how much or how long someone needs a hug. When I first read that, I cried. I also decided that I was going to be that person for someone. If someone hugged me, I would hug them until they let go. I did it with my friends. I did it with my kids. And what I noticed is that hugs got longer.

Allow yourself to be loved by your people. Receive affection fully and without hesitation. So much healing has happened for me because of a simple hug, hand squeeze, or kiss on the forehead. I believe our friends can love us in lots of ways, including the gift of their hugs. So hug them—long.

BELIEVE PEOPLE WHEN THEY SHOW YOU WHO THEY ARE

Maya Angelou famously said, "When someone shows you who they are, believe them the first time." I wish this was a lesson I didn't have to learn the hard way, but it wasn't. My first serious boyfriend after my marriage was a man I thought could maybe be my new forever. It turned out he wasn't who I thought he was. He was duplicitous for much of our relationship, and I painfully ended the relationship. As I started dating again, I was faced with this lesson again in another relationship. Though that person wasn't duplicitous, some of his behaviors were incongruent with who I thought he was. But now that he had shown those actions, I was forced to believe them to be true.

I'm a romantic and an optimist. I love seeing the good in people. I love forgiveness and second chances. But what I have learned is that I can't give more weight to the good than the bad.

If he lies, believe that he is a liar.

If he has a temper with others, believe he will have it with you.

If he is not a gentleman on the first date, he's not a gentleman, period.

I feel like I have learned this lesson more clearly through dating in the past few years than I did at any other time in my life. Dating in my forties is a whole different ball game compared with when I was in college. I want more and will tolerate less. Trusting my gut also means trusting that what has been true in the past will be true in the present. And so, when someone shows me who they are, I believe them.

Of course, this lesson extends far beyond dating, which is why I am sharing this here. I could write the same paragraphs for so many areas of my life. Basically, *trust people when they show you who they are.*

I believe that growth causes you to have less tolerance for things you would have previously put up with. Bad behavior is no longer dismissible. Be aware of this growth and the effect it can have on your relationships with people. Some of the ways you grow may affect your relationships. This might mean that you need to walk away from some relationships in your life. And that walking away is just as important as leaning in to other relationships.

ACCEPT YOUR FRIENDS' LOVE

Without question, my friends have been my saving grace. I once was having a hard, tender day and I called my neighbor Shannon and said, "Can I come over, and will you just give me a hug?" It was early morning, and I knew she was getting her kids ready for school, so I just sat on her front steps and waited. She took those steps two at a time and sat with her arms around me as I cried. I knew I needed to not be alone and I am glad I went to her. Simply having her company for ten minutes gave me the strength to keep moving forward that day.

In the years since my divorce, my friends have witnessed what a spouse has not. The sorrow. The challenges. The wins. The light and the dark. It is my friends I have called to give me courage, strength, and clarity when the road has been so unfamiliar that I have felt I couldn't do it alone.

One time I was doing a Peloton workout and the coach, Robin Arzón, talked about our communities coming around us like midwives, helping us birth our dreams. That visual has stuck with me for years.

You see, midwives delivered my first two children. And for my firstborn, Elias, it was particularly special because there were two midwives there—the midwife who had started the practice and another midwife who was in her fifties and decided to enter the field later in life. She was in training.

I remember both of them caring for me so well during the twenty-four hours they were around (they were working a double). While the teaching midwife took the lead, the other midwife was deeply involved, encouraging me, helping me through contractions, and seeing me through. It was a very long, painful labor, and when I doubted myself, they told me I could do it.

In my own life, I think about the friends in real life who have pushed me onward during the painful season of my divorce and the aftermath. They have been like that senior teaching midwife. They're the ones I've looked to when I have felt uncertainty, celebrated wins, and took steps forward. But others came alongside them, too, similar to that other midwife, close at my side, cheering, and rallying, too.

Together, we birthed a new life for me. It was achingly painful, and I doubted if I could do it, but because of my midwives (my friends), I made it through.

CHAPTER 8

FALLING IN LOVE
WITH YOURSELF

I was about three months into a new relationship. It had gotten serious. We were saying "I love you" and talking about meeting
each other's kids. This man was handsome, kind, intelligent, and
easygoing—a great fit for my passionate, happy personality. I was
enamored. Then one day, we were FaceTiming and a sore spot in the
relationship came up. We had been tap dancing around the issue for
weeks, and he got very upset, more upset than I had ever seen him.
I'll never forget it. He was in a parking lot on FaceTime and started
yelling and cursing at me that I did not understand what he was
going through.

I was gobsmacked. How was this the same gentle, loving man
I had been dating? When he finished his rant, I calmly but firmly
said, "I love myself more than I love you, and I will not be talked to
that way."

He apologized immediately and then apologized again that
night, but a crack was made in our relationship. The relationship
didn't have a strong enough foundation, and we couldn't come back
from it.

Two weeks after that argument, he broke up with me. He said,
"I haven't stopped thinking about what you said to me that day. And

the truth is, I need to work on loving myself before I can be in a relationship." I was heartbroken, but deep in my gut I knew he was right. I deserved better and wanted more than he could give me.

In the moments after that argument and still now, a year later, I think about the Jessica who said, *I love myself more than I love you, and I will not be talked to that way.* Because the truth is, Jessica pre-divorce, pre-counseling, pre-rising, would have not liked being talked to that way, but she probably would have put up with it. My ability to stand firm in what I deserved was a sign of my growth. It also demonstrated to me a kind of self-love that was fresh. I felt confident, brave, and assured in myself in a way that was new.

That breakup also was a catalyst for me to do even more therapeutic work to better understand myself, as well as my relationship and attachment tendencies. I ended up going to a six-day therapy intensive called Onsite.[1] At Onsite, I participated in its Living Centered Workshop, which is for people to focus on self-discovery, healing, and growth through a variety of therapeutic modalities. Each day consists of meditation, lectures, six hours of group therapy, communal activities, and outdoor experiences. While there, you are completely detached from the outside world (no phones, computers, iPads, or televisions are allowed), and the focus is on deep healing and introspective work.

My goal for Onsite was to explore the pain and trauma of my story in a different manner than I previously had and ultimately gain a fresh growth perspective. Onsite requires a significant investment of time, money, and your own full self. It is not something that is easy or fun, but I found it to be deeply rewarding. Going to Onsite was one of the most loving choices I made after my divorce because

---

1. For a free video series that I created with Onsite Clinical Director Ryan Bloch-Snodgrass on moving through disappointment, visit experienceonsite.com/betterthanthis.

it was solely focused on healing from past experiences and deep self-care. They say that an Onsite workshop is equivalent to eight months of therapy in six days, and, based on my experience, I would say that was true. While the work I did there had ripple effects in so many areas of my life, at its core it was about loving myself enough to continue to do work to grow and better myself.

On an episode of *The View*, Joy Behar asked Jennifer Lopez what she learned after experiencing divorce, and she said, "The journey of becoming whole on my own. I always thought that I was going to find happiness and love out—that another person was going to give that to me, and then I realized that's not how it is at all. You actually get to be happy all by yourself...if you can just kind of appreciate yourself and know your worth and your value."[1] One of the greatest lessons I have learned is about being whole on my own. And I think this is something that we all have to learn, whether we are in a relationship or not. We must be secure in the wholeness of ourselves. I believe this wholeness plays out in how we walk through disappointment and grief.

Ultimately, I think a lot of us need to go through an experience of falling in love with ourselves. Think about it. Falling in love with someone is a sacred experience of seeing that person as special and worthy of your affection. It feels too good to be true and like the most miraculous thing. They are the person you think of first thing in the morning and right before you go to bed. You care deeply about their well-being and happiness. They matter to you.

Can you love yourself in that same way? Can you love yourself with an intentionality and affection that demonstrates true care? Loving ourselves is a deeply personal and important practice, and in the aftermath of a disappointment, it is *especially* critical. The words we say to ourselves and the words that we allow others to say to us hold significant weight. The time we invest in ourselves can carry us through hard seasons. We need love from ourselves.

Unfortunately, when disappointment is a part of our stories, it is easy to see ourselves as unlovable or part of the problem we are experiencing. The media shows us that happy people are thin, beautiful, and effortlessly vibrant. They know what to say and how to say it. When life looks less like we imagined, and we look at everything that is wrong, believing lies about ourselves is an easy leap. After all, if I am beautiful, desired, and sexy, shouldn't my life be easier, happier, and going better? Of course, this is toxic thinking, but it is so prevalent in our media that it is very easy to be sucked into the vortex of the lie. Let's unpack some ways to overcome negativity and show ourselves love.

LOVING OUR BODIES

I don't remember a time when I didn't wrestle with body image issues. When I was about ten, a family member pushed on my stomach and told me I should suck in my stomach for the group photo we were taking. It was then that I learned that smaller and flatter was best. Looking back, I can see how that family member was coming from a place with her own body image issues, but I also can't deny the damage that was done with that comment.

When puberty hit and I was nothing but curves, I saw myself as fat and less than. My boobs were too big. My stomach was still too soft (I was ninety-seven pounds when I graduated from high school). In college I gained the freshman fifteen and continued to hate my body. It didn't go as far as an eating disorder, but it was a constant monologue in my head that my body was not good enough.

Once I got married and started having kids, my body changed again. My curves got curvier, my stomach softer and rounder. I had extremely difficult pregnancies, and I gained fifty to sixty pounds each time. Losing the weight was harder with each child. I fought the lies in my head that told me I wasn't pretty anymore. Though my husband told me I was beautiful, he was also going through his own journey. Our intimacy decreased, and I felt certain my body was to blame.

Maybe five years before my marriage ended, I saw a friend who had boudoir photos taken. She looked confident and beautiful. I wanted to feel like she looked. Maybe it would be something I could do and feel, too? I asked my husband if he'd ever want them as a gift, and he told me he thought it was kind of a weird gift. That ended that. Why would I get photos of myself in lingerie if my husband wouldn't even want them? Again, it was easy for me to believe I wasn't desirable or attractive.

About two years after my divorce, I was doing a lot of work around how I saw myself and my body. I revisited the idea of boudoir photos, and it seemed like a good idea. After all, the narrative I told myself in my marriage wasn't true. It wasn't that the photos would have been a weird gift, but that my husband was attracted to men. I wasn't dating anyone, but what if I did them just for me? I deserved to feel beautiful and sexy. I didn't need a man to say that I was worthy to mean I was worthy.

I messaged a well-established photographer in Nashville who specialized in boudoir, and while she normally had a six-month waiting list, she had one spot open in a few weeks. Would I like it? I said yes, paid my deposit, and started shopping for lingerie.

The day of the shoot, it was raining. The location was about an hour away, and I remember feeling both excited and nervous as I drove. What would it be like to have someone take photos of me in lingerie? How would I look? Would I be nervous? Could I be sexy on camera?

I entered the studio with a small bag of lingerie, and the photographer, Rachel, had me spread the lacy garments across the bed.

We talked about what I felt most comfortable in and what I liked best. I liked the white lace two-piece best. We made a plan and I got dressed…well, undressed, then dressed again.

Music played, and over the next two hours, Rachel made me laugh and blush with her words of encouragement. She made me feel sexy, empowered, and desirable. She shrieked with delight as she photographed me, giving me the courage to be fully myself in the photos—a woman comfortable in her body, desirable, sexy, and whole. I'd pose and she'd shoot, then she'd show me the camera, saying, "Look at you! *Look at you.*"

Two hours later, I pulled out of her studio driveway feeling changed. I had done something new and empowering. Being photographed in bits of lace changed me in the best way because it allowed me to see myself as wholly desirable—just as I was. I didn't need to be thinner, flatter, or smaller to be sexy.

When the photos arrived in my inbox, I clicked the link with bated breath. Would I look okay? Was the shoot worth the effort?

It was. I saw a woman that I had never seen before. She was curvy and so beautiful. She was full of light and love and sexy as hell.

She was me.

And it made me cry.

THE STORY OF MY BODY

One of the biggest lessons I have learned in my journey through disappointment is that the way we see our bodies and speak about them, both to ourselves and to others, really matters. Despite the body positivity movement, I struggled with believing that my body would be wanted after my divorce. Actually, I struggled with it during my marriage, too. I liked the idea of body positivity, but I had trouble fully embracing it consistently.

When I began dating, I was hypersensitive to the lie that my body might not be "good enough" for the men I dated. If they were divorced, I would scan their social media to compare myself to their ex-wives. While I was very confident in who I was as a person, my intelligence, my wit, my career, and who I am as a mother, when it came to my body, my head was filled with doubts.

Early into dating, I dated a man named Josh for a few weeks. He was the kind of guy who dripped sex appeal, and he intimidated me a bit. About a week into texting, he said, "I notice you tell me things you think may be negative about your body. You don't need to. Every scar, wrinkle, curve, everything has a story that made you, you. Because of that I will find each one sexy because I am stupidly attracted to the person you are today, which is a product of each of those stories."

A month later, I told him how much those words had meant to me. He told me he thinks most men feel this way. He cited his best friend talking about his wife's body and how he loved it more after children because of what it had been through and meant. I was incredulous. I thought most men wanted women with size 2 pants, tight stomachs, and flawless skin. I had seen men on dating apps list a particular BMI as a requirement for who they would date, which only heightened my insecurity that I was less than desirable.

When my husband didn't seem to desire me, I thought my body was the reason. But what this man was telling me was something different. Not only was it different, but it was healthy, better, good, and true.

If I am honest with you, it's been two years since he texted me that, and writing this section still causes a lump to form in my throat. Do I truly believe what he said to me? Not just believe that it was true for him, but that it is true, period? Most days, yes, but some days, not really. Which shows me that I have grown, but I am also still growing.

His words helped me to go from being mostly unsure about my body to having a renewed confidence. He helped me remember and relearn that my body is not something to hate. My body tells the story of a life lived fully—three children, health challenges and healing, good food, and strength training. Every curve, every scar, every dimple, every wrinkle. My body is the carrier of my heart and soul and should be fully cherished and accepted, by both me and whoever someday might love me.

Your body is the same. Whatever your size. Whatever your shape. Whatever your age. Your body tells the story of you, and every one of our stories is worthy of being loved. And so, speak kindly of your body. She has kept you safe. She knows every part of you. She is beautiful.

LOVING YOURSELF

For Valentine's Day in 2024, I hosted a favorite things party for a bunch of friends. In case you aren't familiar with the concept, a favorite things party is a party where everyone wraps up and brings three of their favorite things, and then you do a gift exchange. Everyone goes home with three great gifts. I love gathering around the table, so for my party I planned a full homemade meal with Italian soup, salad, garlic bread, and cherry cheesecake to enjoy before the gift exchange.

I invited friends from different facets of my life. The guest list included former coworkers, friends from church, and moms of some of my kids' friends. Every person only knew a few others in the room, so I had everybody introduce themselves, say how they knew each other, and then say one thing they loved about themselves. I didn't think saying something that they loved about themselves was a hard prompt, but for many of the women it was incredibly difficult. One of my friends said she couldn't name anything and begged to move on from the introduction.

After the party, I texted her and said, "I didn't want to embarrass you, but I think you are one of the most genuinely kind people I know. Truly. You are easy to talk to, nonjudgmental, safe, warm, and lovely. You should be able to rattle off a long list. You are amazing!"

She replied and said, "Aw you are too kind!! Thanks for filling my bucket. It's really kind of obnoxious that I couldn't just say something." I didn't think it was obnoxious, but it did make me ache a bit because I know that many women would feel the same way.

Loving ourselves can feel challenging because of relationships we have had in the past, lies from others we have believed, what we see in the media, and so much more. Just like it takes work to love someone else, it takes work to love ourselves. Today, get out a pad of paper and make a long list of what you love about yourself. Think about:

- What you love about yourself physically
- What you love about yourself mentally
- What you love about yourself emotionally
- What you love about how you are with other people
- What you love about the way you work
- What you love about how you are with those close to you
- What you love about your gifts

I realize this is much easier said than done. Parts of your story may make it hard to love yourself in certain areas. This may be something that you will want to talk through with your therapist. Our love for ourselves should be vast and deep. We are the only person that we will be with our entire lives. To love ourselves is to fully accept, fully desire, and fully cherish the wholeness of personhood, flesh and bone, heart and soul. It is no small thing to say I am fully and completely worth loving.

When we show ourselves that kind of love, other actions like growth, healing, and acceptance become easier. Think about the people you love most in the world. Maybe it is your spouse, your parents, your kids, or a very close friend. When you think about these people, you don't immediately think of their flaws, but their love, their presence, the way they make your heart beat a little faster. Likewise, when you think about yourself, look at yourself the way I looked at my friend and the way those people you love most look at you.

I'll never forget when a man I was dating said, "You are a unicorn." Though I wasn't the unicorn for him, it shifted the way I saw myself in the dating world. I was no longer maybe not good enough; instead, I was incredibly rare. A gift to be with. Magical.

You are a unicorn. You are awesome, unique, and one of a kind. Do not let the disappointment of your circumstances and/or doubt in yourself cloud your perspective. Be full of love and hope for all that lies ahead for you.

CARING FOR MYSELF

After I got home from a winter trip to visit my family in Wisconsin, Matthew met the kids and me at my house to help empty out the car, celebrate Ezra's birthday, and eat dinner with us, which he had prepared in advance of our arrival. It was really kind and helped transition all of us home from the trip.

The kids then went back to Matthew's house, and I was left alone in a quiet house. If you are married with children, you might think this sounds glorious, but I assure you, it hits differently when you are divorced—even if you have a really great relationship with your ex.

I knew I needed a gentle night. I watched a show, took a long bath, listened to my audiobook, lit a candle, and put freshly washed sheets on my bed. Could the sheets have waited? Sure. But also no.

You see, when we were married, whenever I would come home from a trip, Matthew would have clean sheets on the bed. I *love* clean sheets. (Did you know Jackie Kennedy Onassis had her sheets changed daily? That's a bit much, but I understand and appreciate her deep love of clean sheets, too.) It was such a tender way to show care, and I was delighted every single time.

So that night, putting clean sheets on my bed was an act of loving myself well. The process of making the bed *for me and only me* after a trip was deeply significant. Sometimes, there are things we can do only for ourselves. It might be getting on that bike, eating or not eating a certain food, making a doctor's appointment, or pursuing a hobby. Or it might be putting clean sheets on your bed when no one else is there to do it.

When we make the choice to actively care for ourselves, we experience wholeness, vibrancy, and light in a deeply meaningful way. On that night, I was reminded of that as I smoothed out my bedding and got ready for bed. Consider ways you might actively care for yourself, especially in seasons of turmoil and healing.

HAVE A GROWTH MINDSET

One of the benefits of my divorce is that it shifted my mindset to how can I grow and become a healthier, better, and more aware person. Yes, my marriage ended because my husband was gay, but that doesn't mean that our marriage was otherwise perfect or that I couldn't have done certain things better. My initial focus was on the immediate bleeding of the loss of Matthew, but then it shifted. I started to look at things like my attachment style, codependency, my own self-care, and more.

In John Stamos's memoir, *If You Would Have Told Me*, he writes about his divorce from Rebecca Romijn and how afterward he found himself in rehab.[2] During a meeting, he wrote down the things that had happened that led to the divorce. His list was all Rebecca. Then the facilitator said to him, "Now write down how you played a role in it." It was a light bulb moment for him. He saw that he had played a much bigger role than he had given himself credit for.

It would have been detrimental to me and my future relationships if I didn't take time to evaluate myself and my habits within my marriage. Someone who has a growth mindset is focused on learning and growing. In the book *Emotional Intelligence Habits*, Travis Bradberry writes, "A growth mindset is more than just a frame of mind. It's an unwavering belief in your ability to reach your goals."[3] When you are considering ways to grow, ask yourself questions like:

- What is an area where I feel stuck? What can I do to get unstuck?
- What "script" have I been following, and how can I rewrite it?
- What actions can I take to get me to where I want to go?
- What do I complain about? Is that complaint pointing to something I need to work on or change?

Having a growth mindset doesn't mean you won't make mistakes. We all make mistakes. But when someone is living from a growth mindset perspective, they look at the mistakes as opportunities to grow.

Your growth mindset might have a different frame of reference in terms of growth, but the desire to not stay where you are is a universal one worth adopting. It shows maturity to say, "I have been living one way, behaving one way, or thinking one way for a long time, and maybe there is another way of living, behaving, or thinking." That is transforming your mindset from a fixed mindset to a growth mindset. And doing so will help you to create a life you love.

BELIEVING IN YOUR WORTHINESS

I'll never forget a therapy session when I brought one of those giant Post-it pads with me. I walked in the door, and Stephanie looked from me to the Post-its and said with smile, "Okay, what do you have in mind?" I said, "We are going to look at every guy I have dated and see what I have learned and what I still need to learn." I stuck the pages on the plaster walls of her office and began to talk, write, and tear up.

For forty-five minutes I wrote on those pages. I wrote the men's names and what each taught me about what I wanted and didn't want in a partner. The men had taught me things about chemistry, intimacy, and fun, and opened my eyes to possibilities in relationships that I didn't expect. They also showed me character traits that were not compatible with me and my values. Those yellow sticky pages filled quickly.

I also had another big sheet that said "What I Have Learned" across the top. On it, Stephanie had me write what I learned about myself. The biggest lesson was that I was worthy of love.

When I got divorced, I wouldn't have been able to articulate what that meant. I think if someone would have asked me, "Are you worthy of love?" I would have quickly replied yes. But if I had sat with it, I would have needed to admit that the worthiness I was agreeing to had a lot of qualifiers. I needed answers to these questions: What was love in the confines of a marriage? How did I define worthiness? What were the limitations I put on those words? Most importantly, did I really believe in my own worthiness, or just in the idea of worthiness?

My husband did love me, as best he could. But because of his own trauma and story, our love ultimately wasn't the kind of love either of us wanted in a marriage. We both had stories that affected how we showed up for each other. And when our marriage ended, I had to face my own shortcomings. I had a choice: Would I allow myself to believe *I am who I am and I cannot change?* Or would I look inward and grow?

As I dated, I began to unpack what being worthy of love meant. And that unpacking led me to seriously consider other areas of my life where I had a limited view of my own worthiness. I realized that my self-worth was causing me to limit my imagination for the future and what could be possible for me. I would think things like:

I'm too fat to be loved by someone like that.

I'm never going to find someone who will love this in me.

There's something wrong with me, because I keep experiencing breakups.

Maybe I'm not worthy of love again.

Oof. That last sentence. *Maybe I'm not worthy of love again.* Gosh, that's an awful thing to write, and truthfully, it's even more awful to believe. But I believed it. I'm thankful I don't anymore. You see, I finally accepted that worthiness is a birthright. We are all worthy of every good thing. Worth isn't based on personality, finances, the "right" job, or how attractive we are. Someone isn't worth more or less based on the color of their skin, where they live, or what they believe.

At the beginning of Jamie Kern Lima's book *Worthy*, she says, "In life, you don't soar to the level of your hopes and dreams, you stay stuck at the level of your self-worth. You don't rise to what you believe is possible, you fall to what you believe you're worthy of."[4]

The deepest work you can do to achieve your goals and reframe the trajectory of your life is around worthiness. The love you give others will only be matched by the love you show yourself. In the Bible, I love that the greatest commandment Jesus gives is to love your neighbor as you love yourself. He is saying that very thing: the love you give your neighbors will be reflective of the love you show yourself. And the worthiness you believe for yourself is directly tied to that.

What lies do you believe around your self-worth? What reframing do you need to do? How is this self-worth tied to the disappointment(s) in your life? Have others in your life contributed to a limited or negative view of your self-worth, and if so, who and how?

These few questions have the power to create a transformational shift in your life. The sooner you embrace the depth of your self-worth, the higher you will soar. You *are* worthy.

You are worthy of love.

You are worthy of hope.

You are worthy of goodness.

You are worthy of peace.

You are worthy of possibility.

You are worthy of your dreams.

WHAT'S TRUE ABOUT YOU

When disappointment is blanketing our lives, it is much easier to grab hold of the negative and write that story as true. The chart-topping song "You Say" by Lauren Daigle was released during the time Matthew and I were deep in therapy but he hadn't come out yet. In the subsequent months, as everything unraveled, I listened to that song every day. The lyrics include:

I keep fighting voices in my mind that say I'm not
   enough
Every single lie that tells me I will never measure up
You say I am loved when I can't feel a thing
You say I am strong when I think I am weak

During times of disappointment, finding true statements to cling to can be a lifeline. What are things about yourself that are true, even in this devastating, frustrating, tumultuous time? Looking to Scripture and songs like "You Say" were helpful for me, but maybe words from a trusted family member, friend, or therapist can help you. What matters is that you have a truthful narrative to reflect on when you start to tell yourself lies during this hard time. Make a list of those truths. Tack them up on a mirror.

I am loved.

I am strong.

I am held.

I belong.

What would be on your list?

I am _____

I am _____

I am _____

I am _____

In researching for this book, I found a well-respected study by Fred Luskin of Stanford University, who asserts that we have an average of sixty thousand thoughts a day and that the large majority of those thoughts (for most people) are negative and repetitive.[5] When I read this, I thought about the negative things that run through my head and how many can be self-directed, such as how I look, what I didn't accomplish, ways I could be a better parent, and more. This negativity adds up, and it can color our perspective in a negative way.

When my kids say something untrue about themselves, such as "I'm dumb," I am quick to reply, "Don't talk about my friend that way!" It makes them smile and gives us a chance to reframe the struggle or the situation. The hard truth is that we often say things about ourselves that we would never say to friends or family. If you find yourself caught in a cycle of negative thinking, consider doing the following:

- **Be curious.** What is informing that thought? Sit with it and try to understand it.
- **Pay attention to patterns.** If you are thinking the same thoughts daily, look for the why. What is the history? Is it something that is all-consuming? I heard a therapist at Onsite say, "If it is hysterical, it's historical," meaning if it is something that is emphasized with intensity, an underlying history probably exists and is likely why it keeps popping up.
- **Redirect where you're thinking.** Talk to yourself the way you would talk to someone you love. Remind yourself that you would not talk to a friend that way, and likewise, you shouldn't talk to yourself in that manner.
- **Consider others who may affect your narrative.** Is there anyone in your life who is contributing to your thoughts and perspective? It might be that you need to

have a conversation with them or change the way you interact with them. And if they are no longer in your life but are still informing your inner monologue, that points to some historical work you probably need to do in therapy.

- **Speak positively to yourself.** This is probably the simplest thing on this list. Start speaking positively. Change your framing to be positive instead of negative. If necessary, grab some Post-its, write affirmations on them, and place them where you will see them every day. You are worth goodness, and it starts inside with how you see yourself.

Our words have weight, and the narratives that run through our heads become truths that we believe. We must consciously choose to reframe to become better versions of ourselves. Doing so will change not only your life but the lives of those who know you.

CHAPTER 9

NOURISHING YOURSELF AND MOVING YOUR BODY

When Matthew left, my relationship with food changed. In my marriage, I would yo-yo diet, in part because I wanted to get healthier and feel better, and in part because I wanted to be desirable for my husband. When my marriage ended and I had no one, I ate whatever I wanted, at whatever time. This was especially true when my kids were at their dad's. It was not unusual for me to snack at ten o'clock at night, grazing on whatever was accessible. I ignored all the things I knew about food and living a healthy life. Instead, I wanted instant gratification. I didn't drink or do drugs; I did sugar. I needed the hit.

A year later, I was the heaviest I had ever been besides those postpartum months after having babies. Every day I thought about how fat I was and told myself I needed to change my habits, do better, look better, be better. Then I would snack on chips and candy, have dessert every night, and tell myself that I deserved it.

Please know this: food was not the problem. It was my relationship to it and to myself that was the problem.

One morning, before getting in the shower, I looked at my naked body in my bathroom mirror. I noticed her softness, every curve. I got in the shower and cried. It hit me hard how I had been treating her and why.

That morning, I looked at myself and saw what I was doing. I contacted a nutritionist named Amy Williams, knowing I needed accountability and a different path forward. In our first meeting, I cried when I talked about the way I saw myself and my body. In the weeks that followed, I became a different person because instead of using food to cope, I was using food to energize. I learned what affected my blood sugar and why I would crash in the afternoons. I was able to get my weight under control and saw all my bloodwork improve.

I talked to Amy about the benefits of focusing on nutrition during hard seasons, and here's what she had to say: "Many of my clients lead busy lives with stressful jobs and a handful of kids. When going through seasons of being extra busy or stressed, focusing on proper nourishment has a never-ending list of benefits. Some of those include being able to handle the stress better, more mental clarity and less brain fog, more energy to endure the busy season, happier mood and less anxiety, more focused on tasks at hand, and being able to recover better and faster."

I know it feels counterintuitive, but not focusing on proper nourishment has a negative effect. Amy went on to add, "When clients don't focus on proper nourishment during stressful periods, the complete opposite happens: they are tired, frustrated, moody, clouded, and unable to perform their jobs as easily or efficiently. So, make sure you always focus on nourishing your body, especially during a busy or challenging season. Eating properly seems so small, but in fact, it has more of a profound impact than we give it credit for."

It's possible that you, too, may be hindering your healing because of your relationship with food. Wherever you are in your journey, take a look at what you are eating and your eating habits. Ask yourself these questions:

- Am I nourishing myself in a way that is healthy?
- Am I eating foods that may be negatively contributing to how I feel?

- Am I eating too much, too little, or just the right amount of food to feel good?
- Are there choices I could make to help encourage healthy eating (such as less eating out, less sugar, more whole foods, etc.)?

Also, consider keeping a food journal for a week. Write down everything you eat and drink, the times you ate, your hunger level, and notes about your mood. Be honest in your tracking. This is a judgment-free zone. At the end of the week, ask yourself:

- Was I consistent with my eating?
- Am I eating more or less than I should be?
- How did I feel this week physically and emotionally?
- How did the foods I ate contribute to my energy? (For instance, on a day that you ate a lot of refined sugar and carbs, did you feel more sluggish?)

You might notice some habits that you want to refine as you work to nourish your body. Also, if you have a doctor's appointment scheduled, consider bringing your food journal to discuss ways you can be taking the best nutritional care of yourself. This is not about dieting but about eating in the best way possible so that you can feel your best. When you feel your best, you will do your best and be your best. It is that simple.

MOVEMENT

Do you know what a limiting belief is? A limiting belief is something that we hold on to that limits us in some way. In Jamie Kern Lima's book *Worthy*, she writes, "Limiting beliefs can be taught to us or learned over time, and sometimes we're not even aware we have them. These limiting beliefs make up the portion of our belief system…that can hold us back, keep us stuck, and fill our minds with fear and self-doubt. While we believe them to be true, they can often be completely made-up stories we tell ourselves, or have been taught, that are in fact not true at all."[1] In short, limiting beliefs hold all of us back. Identifying what they are and then turning them upside down is an important task in the path of freedom.

A limiting belief that I have held on to is that I am not athletic. I believe this started when I was a kid, when people would compare my sister and me. My sister had a natural knack for sports. She was a gymnast, a volleyball player, and a pole vaulter. I didn't have any interest in these things, instead gravitating toward theater, music, reading, and writing. It was easy for people to affirm the narrative of the athlete and the bookworm. It wasn't meant to be harmful, but looking back I see how I carried that story throughout my life.

Last one picked for teams in gym class.
I'm not an athlete.

Comparing my sister's abs to my soft belly.
I'm not an athlete.

Trying a yoga class and feeling lost the whole time.
I'm not an athlete.

Getting out of breath as I try out jogging.
I'm not an athlete.

Over time, my lifestyle became more sedentary. I didn't move my body because I didn't like exercise and I have never been an athlete. It's just not my thing. Never has been. Never will be. Or so I thought.

During the pandemic, like everyone else in the world, I was stir-crazy. So the kids and I would go for walks. Then I saw on social media more and more people talking about these Peloton bikes they were riding. I had never tried cycling, but I saw others doing it and thought maybe I could, too. It was the first whisper in a long time that made me think that maybe I could do something athletic.

I ordered a bike and got it set up. I logged in to my first class, and it. was. hard. But I wasn't going to quit. I kept taking classes. I hung a giant Post-it on the wall and started to write down things that the coaches said in the classes. I believed in myself.

At the end of my first year, I was ranked in the top 10 percent of all Peloton users for amount of time spent in the app. I realized that I was an athlete. Me. The girl who hates running and was always picked last in gym class. Being an athlete has nothing to do with skill and everything to do with mindset.

Movement made more than my body stronger; it made my mind and soul stronger. Research has long shown that movement is medicine. I think if I had learned that at a young age instead of tying movement to being an "athlete," my life would have benefited greatly. But better late than never!

When you are going through a great change or disappointment, moving your body is critical to helping yourself manage what you are carrying emotionally. According to a study by Ashish Sharma, Vishal Madaan, and Frederick D. Petty,[2] "Health benefits from regular exercise that should be emphasized and reinforced by every mental health professional to their patients include the following:

1. Improved sleep
2. Increased interest in sex

3. Better endurance
4. Stress relief
5. Improvement in mood
6. Increased energy and stamina
7. Reduced tiredness that can increase mental alertness
8. Weight reduction
9. Reduced cholesterol and improved cardiovascular fitness"

Though this was written nearly twenty years ago, countless research studies since have supported these findings. You must make time to move your body, no matter how much pressure you are under, no matter how much you don't feel like it, no matter what your time constraints are. Even if you fit in only ten minutes in the morning, ten minutes in the middle of the day, and ten minutes in the evening, you will be able to manage better if you are giving yourself the gift of movement.

I had read these findings and knew these facts for much of my adulthood, but it wasn't until I went through the pandemic and my divorce that I really leaned in and believed. My life was transformed when I made movement a regular habit.

If you are someone who struggles with movement, here are a few practical ways you can try to incorporate it into your life:

- **Ask a friend to be your movement buddy.** Do you have a neighbor, coworker, or friend who would be willing to go on a walk with you?
- **Join a gym or class.** Paying for classes can be very motivating, because if you are paying for something, you are more likely to want to be sure you aren't wasting your financial resources.
- **Schedule it.** Something that is on your schedule is less likely to be canceled. Schedule movement the same way you would schedule meetings and appointments.

- **Do it with your kids.** If you have children, move together. Go for walks after dinner. Play outside. You'll be building memories and connections and getting that movement in.
- **Start small.** You don't need to buy a home gym to move your body. Find a fitness video on YouTube or sign up for classes through Peloton, Apple TV+, or a similar service.
- **Believe in yourself.** For so long, I didn't believe I could, so I didn't. But once I started cycling, I started to believe I could. And then because I believed it, I did it. Try listening to the voice in your head that says you can, and then do it.

REST

Rest is something I have always struggled to prioritize. My nickname has long been the Energizer Bunny. I keep going, and going, and going. But eventually, even batteries wear out. One of the biggest lessons of my life is that my body needs rest. I'm not talking about sleep, though we are going to get there as well. I am talking about the idea of taking breaks and resting.

One of my favorite things to do is read. Because I have been on a book deadline, I have been working longer days to keep everything in the air—this project, my regular content creator work, kids, travel, and so on. Consequently, I have not been reading as much. I have been feeling the effects of not slowing down enough to read, and so this weekend, I put everything aside and got lost in a good book. I devoured a mystery in a day and a half and started the week energized to get back into it.

That's what rest does. It ensures that we can be our best by filling us up. You have surely heard of the oxygen mask philosophy, right? On an airplane, the flight attendants always say to put

139

your oxygen mask on first, before helping children and others nearby. This is because you can't help others if you don't take care of yourself first. Rest is the oxygen that you need to keep moving forward.

One of my favorite books on rest is *Sabbath* by Wayne Muller, a twenty-five-year-old book that is as relevant today as it was when it was released.[3] I have read the book multiple times, trying to soak in Muller's wisdom, which often rubs against my often crazy pace of life. In it he says, "The Sabbath is a revolutionary invitation to consider that the fruits of our labor may be found in the restful and unhurried harvest of time. In time, we can taste the sweetness of peace, serenity, well-being, and delight." Later in the book, he writes, "The Sabbath is a patch of ground secured by a tiny fence, when we withdraw from the endless choices afforded us and listen, uncover what is ultimately important, remember what is quietly sacred. Sabbath restrictions on work and activity actually create a space of great freedom; without these self-imposed restrictions, we may never be truly free."

When we are rebuilding and/or healing after disappointment, we might be tempted to stay busy. Some people might even advise that being busy is a great catalyst for healing because if our minds and hearts are distracted, we won't focus on what we have lost or experienced. I don't disagree with this as a short-term solution. As I shared earlier, after my divorce, I worked tirelessly on my online platform, trying to grow my business and stay distracted. Eventually though, I burned out. I needed to rest and recharge. I needed Sabbath.

Take a look at the way you spend your time. Are you in a season of staying busy or are you intentionally practicing a Sabbath rest? If not, where can you say no so that you can say yes to yourself? Like Muller writes, creating a fence around our time so that we can rest can yield much growth and healing.

SLEEP

As a mother, one of my cure-alls for my kids is sleep.

You're grumpy? Take a nap.

Finding it hard to focus? You didn't sleep enough last night. Go to bed.

Been up too late all weekend? Tonight you need to go to bed early.

"You need sleep," I say to my kids, and they whine and protest before falling into a deep slumber. And the next morning they are like different people. My youngest son will wake up early no matter what time he goes to bed, so I had his pediatrician talk to him about sleep being important to his body because he didn't believe me.

Sleep isn't just necessary for kids, though. We all need sleep, and sleep is directly correlated to health—physical and mental. Study after study point to the ways we are benefited by sleep. It regulates our mood, improves our food cravings, helps with brain health, and so much more.

Our sleep is often affected during hard seasons. During that nine-month period when Matthew and I were in limbo, he would often wake up during the night and get out of bed. Every time he would rise, I would wake, too. Instantly, my brain would start catastrophizing, wondering, *What is he thinking? Is he upset about something? Can I fix it?* We'd both fall back to sleep eventually, but that interrupted sleep made the season especially difficult because fatigue is so negatively pervasive to our systems and lives.

When my daughter was a baby, she was a terrible sleeper. She and I both didn't sleep for much of her first year. Once she started sleeping and I started sleeping, too, I felt like a different person. I would go to work and feel like I was showing up for my job as wholly myself for the first time in a year. It was that dramatic.

You also might find that you are filling your days with so much or that you are so emotionally taxed that you shortchange your sleep so that you can get more done. I have certainly done this. In the months after Matthew moved out, when I still had a day job and was juggling influencer work, I would often start working early in the morning, then work my day job, then work again multiple hours at night. I was burning the candle at both ends, as the saying goes, and felt really depleted. It's not news to state that lack of sleep has a massive effect on our work productivity. In fact, research shows that "fatigue-related productivity losses were estimated to cost $1967/employee annually."[4]

Here are six things that have helped me improve my sleep:

- **Create a sleep routine.** There is no one perfect sleep routine, but creating a habit of preparing your body for sleep is very effective. For instance, you might put on pajamas, wash your face, brush your teeth, read for thirty minutes, and then listen to a short meditation before going to sleep.
- **Turn off those screens.** Blue light has a negative effect on the melatonin our body produces, so it is recommended to turn off screens at least thirty minutes before bed.
- **Avoid caffeine and alcohol before bed.** This tip might seem obvious, but for ideal rest, avoid these to ensure you get deep sleep.
- **Exercise.** Yes, exercise during the day will help you sleep better at night.
- **Cool down the temperature.** According to SleepFoundation.org, you will sleep better in a cold environment, so set your thermostat to 65–68 degrees Fahrenheit for the best sleep.[5]
- **Practice sound masking.** Use a white noise machine to mask sounds that may interrupt your sleep. One study

also showed that people who use white noise tend to fall asleep faster and sleep deeper.[6]

In *The Sleep Revolution: Transforming Your Life, One Night at a Time*, Arianna Huffington writes, "[Sleep] makes us better at things our culture celebrates—performing and doing—it also teaches us how to trust and let go. As our days become more and more consumed by doing, by distractions and urgency, sleep, waiting for us every night, offers a surrender."[7] I love that picture of surrender because it is one that I know I need to cling to more often than I do.

If you are in a season of grief, you might struggle to sleep. And if you are in a season of rebuilding, you might think it counterproductive to stop the building to rest. But in both cases, sleep is what your body needs. It will give you the fuel and the fire to endure and be made new. Make it a priority so that you can be who you need to be in this season.

Our family went on a cruise in 2023, and it was amazing. As is the case on cruises, there was all-you-can-eat food, especially french fries and ice cream. My kids thought it was the best thing ever. We also had incredible ports of call that were amazing to experience but left us exhausted. By the end of seven days, we needed a vacation from our vacation. We had not slept enough and had clearly eaten too much junk, thanks to endless buffets of french fries and ice cream. We needed a reset.

Just like after that cruise, our bodies often tell us when we need to improve our habits. We will be cranky, tired, headachy, and so on. But as we make changes, we will see improvements, and these improvements help every area of our lives, internally and externally. The ways that you nourish your body will contribute to your future health and happiness as you rebuild a life you love. This work is the work that few see but makes a big difference. You must make your health a priority by moving, eating well, resting, and sleeping.

Create a report card for the different areas discussed in this chapter. What areas are you doing well in, and what could use a little work? Use this report card as a guide as you move forward. Give yourself a letter grade and write some comments about areas where you are doing well and where you have opportunity for growth.

Area of focus	Letter grade	Successes	Growth opportunities
Food			
Movement			
Rest			
Sleep			

CHAPTER 10

STEPPING INTO
NEW EXPERIENCES

Matthew had just moved out, and I needed my family and time away. I didn't want to be in my house that reminded me so much of what I had lost and the unknown road ahead. Remember, this was June 2020, so COVID-19 was rampant. We were not yet gathering very much. But with everything going on, my family agreed that we had to get together. The trouble was, I didn't feel comfortable flying, so I had to drive my three kids by myself to Wisconsin—a ten-hour drive without stops.

Previously, the longest road trip I had ever done alone with the kids was to Atlanta, a short four hours from Nashville. The Wisconsin trip felt daunting. I remember talking with my friend Jo, and she recalled her first road trip from Nashville to Michigan after her divorce. "I was so nervous! But now, I can do that trip with my eyes closed. You are going to do great." Her encouragement and perspective were so valuable to me.

The kids and I piled in the car with lots of DVDs and snacks to make the trip easy for the kids. They were twelve, nine, and five at the time. I put my sister's Wisconsin address into my navigation app and began the drive north. It was a sunny but long day. We made frequent stops. I listened to audiobooks and talked to friends and family on the phone. Eventually, around dinnertime, I stepped into my sister's house. She wrapped her arms around my neck and I cried. I had made it.

A week later I did the drive in reverse. And it wasn't as hard as the drive to Wisconsin. I did the drive again in the winter. And then in the summer again. Now I am like Jo. I can do that drive with my eyes closed. Heck, two summers ago, I tacked on a second leg and drove to Canada with the kids to visit my friend Ann at her farm. I was far from the girl who was nervous about driving to another state; now I was driving across international borders.

One of the gifts of disappointment is that you will begin to have new experiences. Some of these are because of the nature of the disappointment, such as road-tripping by yourself instead of with a partner, or starting to date again (more on that in a few pages). Other new experiences result from the freedom that comes from your growth after the disappointment.

All of these experiences will help you to create a life you love. You get to have the agency to say yes, do new things, and believe in yourself in ways you maybe never have before. You will also likely meet new people and try things that your path might not have previously brought you to.

FACING NEW EXPERIENCES

Some new experiences that you are going to face are going to be really nerve-racking. I remember when I was considering whether I was ready to begin dating. I remember talking to my therapist for weeks about it and discussing why I wasn't ready, all the what-ifs, and so on. I read message boards about dating and got more nervous about the prospect. One week, as I was sitting in a session with Stephanie, she said gently, "I think you are ready. And I think it will be good for you."

Because Stephanie is an excellent therapist, she rarely gives any sort of advice. Therapists are there to listen, ask questions, and allow you to discover things on your own. So when Stephanie pointedly said yes, my ears perked up. I knew she was gently nudging because it was the best care she could give me. I also knew that I was not the only person she had provided therapy for who had gone through a divorce, so I could also trust her experience in this area.

And she was right. I was ready. So I downloaded Bumble, created a profile, and went live. Like the trip to Wisconsin, at first it was really uncomfortable. I was nervous. I didn't know if I could do it. I'll never forget the first man I kissed after the divorce.

I heard his car in the driveway before I saw him. We met on a dating app and had been texting and FaceTiming for several weeks. But due to my son getting COVID, and then me catching it, we had to wait to meet in person. For our first date, we decided to meet at my house for breakfast, which would be a more comfortable and intimate atmosphere than a restaurant. (Yes, my *Dateline*-loving friend was worried he might be a serial killer, but I felt confident it was going to be okay.)

My heart pounded as he got out of the silver car and I noticed the fit of his shirt on his athletic arms, the confident swagger in his step, and the smile across his face. I was nervously standing on my porch, a smile on my face and my heart pounding in my throat. This was going to happen. I was about to be kissed. I had not kissed anyone besides my ex-husband in nearly twenty years. Would I remember how?

He stepped up to meet me, put one arm around my waist and a hand on my face, and pulled me in for a kiss. I felt like I was in a rom-com, in the very best way possible. At that moment, the world stopped. All that mattered was the two of us, finally meeting after endless hours of texts and conversation. His kiss was passionate, purposeful, and exciting, and my body was on fire.

We went into the house, kissing and touching with the hormones of teenagers and the experience of adults. It was exhilarating. Oh, it could be like this? I didn't believe it until it happened. You don't need all the juicy details—I promise, we held to some boundaries!—but that morning changed me. It felt like a very physical example of redemption. Years later, when I think about that kiss, it still gives me butterflies. I think it was in part because, my gosh, the man knew what he was doing, but also in part because it was so incredibly healing.

What I learned from that first post-divorce kiss was that my heart would love again. Though things ended up not working out romantically between me and that man, that doesn't change the lesson I learned from him: love was not going to be a one-time thing for me.

Redemption is part of life. When I was in my pit of despair and devastation was everywhere, it was hard for me to believe that I would climb out of that pit and have a story of redemption. It was simply too hard to fathom starting over, rebuilding, and rediscovering myself.

I'm not one to overspiritualize, but that first kiss was a tangible gift from God. When he left, I sat in the silence of my house, taking time to think about what had just happened. In that moment, I felt God whisper to me, "I never left you. You have always been loved—even without this man's kiss."

We simply cannot stay in the pit forever. Redemption is always possible. We can lean in to hope and love and seek out another way through our circumstances. We may feel alone, but we are never alone. God is always with us.

What new experiences can you have in your life as you rebuild it? Have you given yourself permission to imagine? Consider making a bucket list for this next chapter of your life. What do you want to do? Who do you want to be? How do you want to live?

These are big, big questions. They will take time to authentically answer. But they will provide wisdom on how to spend your time, the work you need to do, and what your heart aches for. You might not know everything yet, but I bet you know more than you realize.

For instance, when I had that first kiss, I didn't know fully what I wanted in a relationship with a new partner. I was still learning who I was as a single woman at forty, what my expectations were of a partner, and what characteristics were and weren't compatible with who I was. Those lessons were only going to come with new experiences. I had to date. I had to be vulnerable with new potential partners. I had to put myself out there so I could learn. Now I can easily give you a list of my red and green flags, and I have a lot of clarity around dating. It still can be daunting, but it is less so because of the clarity and confidence I have gained from past experiences.

LETTING GO OF OLD EXPERIENCES AND TRADITIONS

While you will have new experiences as you rebuild, some of those new experiences will come from letting go of old experiences and traditions. For instance, when I was married, nearly every year, my husband and I would go to see Vince Gill and Amy Grant's Christmas show. This Christmas show is a Nashville tradition and became one for the two of us as well. We would buy tickets in the summer and look forward to the evening together for much of the year. I loved that night, but when we divorced, I knew that I wouldn't be able to go to that show again without Matthew. It was just too tied to him and to us. Instead of making me happy, as it had for so many years, I knew I would get sad sitting there without him by my side.

But I love Christmas and Christmas shows! So I bought tickets to other Christmas shows. I found a new annual show to love and made a tradition of going to that show instead. I still feel nostalgic about Vince and Amy's show, and I believe someday I will be able to go again. But for now, creating new traditions and experiences is what I need. This letting go is part of the healing journey.

If you have experiences that don't work anymore, I think it is important to look at them as experiences from a past season of your life. It isn't that you are being limited now, but rather that you are expanding to create new experiences in this period of your life. I think if Matthew and I had stayed married, we would have had many more Christmases seeing Vince and Amy. Just because I don't have that doesn't make my Christmas season less fun or less meaningful. It just includes different fun and meaningful activities.

I think it can sometimes be easy to fall into the trap of negative thinking around something that can no longer be. We can be bitter, angry, or resentful. But these emotions are not helpful. Instead, be grateful for what was and be grateful for what is to come. This expansive perspective about your life is hopeful and exciting instead of limiting. Very few things are forever. Letting go of the experiences that no longer work in your story is part of your rebuilding. You get to decide what the next experience is.

HABITS

I started biting my nails when I was six years old. My parents tried everything to get me to stop. They tried bitter-tasting nail polish. Bribery. One extended family member used shame tactics: "Pretty girls don't bite their nails. Don't you want to be pretty?" I repeatedly failed. Nothing could stop me from mindlessly chewing my nails. Eventually they gave up.

As an adult, I continued the habit, even though I hated it. I hated how my hands looked. I hated when I would notice others looking at my hands. Finally, I started getting manicures. It was the only way to not bite my nails. I didn't hate my hands anymore. In fact, I loved them. I loved picking new colors and I loved that something I had been self-conscious about for more than thirty years finally was no longer a thing.

While nail biting is probably not something contributing to a major life disappointment, I think it is a good example of how many habits we practice that we do mindlessly. It is just how we live, act, work, speak, and so on. Habits can contribute to our lives in positive and negative ways, causing us to have positive and negative experiences, some of which might happen routinely. As we work to rebuild our lives, taking a personal inventory of our habits can be helpful. Ask yourself:

- What habits do I have related to how I care for myself?
- What habits do I have at work?
- What habits do I have at home?
- What habits do I have in intimate relationships?
- What habits do I have in how I parent?
- What habits do I have with my friends?

These are very broad questions, but hopefully they might spark some thoughts around habits you have that need to be examined. For instance, when I got divorced, I started to realize that some of the overfunctioning that I did in my marriage was not helpful in our relationship. I would come into a situation, completely take over, and leave little room for my husband to contribute. Over time it led to him checking out and me carrying more than I should have in the relationship. As I entered new relationships, I sought to have more equal engagement around planning and decision-making so that history would not repeat itself.

In his bestselling book *Atomic Habits*, James Clear talks about how scoring our habits with a + (good), – (bad), or = (neutral) can help develop awareness around our habits.[1] He notes that habits are not really good or bad, but that it's more about labeling their effectiveness. As you go through the process of evaluating your own through the context of a disappointment, look at them through the lens of how they contribute to rebuilding a life that you love.

For instance, when I started dating, I was so excited about the possibility of every new partner. I would quickly go too deep. I was *not* casual. I think this was partly because I love to go deep and really get to know people and partly because I had been doing so much therapy on myself that nothing was casual and light for me. I didn't want to waste time on someone who wasn't a good match. After several relationships, my therapist and I talked about how this habit was causing dates to get overwhelmed and the relationship and me to feel like I was too much. It wasn't that my habit to go deep was bad, but it wasn't effective in cultivating a lasting relationship. I learned to shift my conversation and questions for the first few dates to better reflect where we were (the very beginning) and honor the process.

In *The Power of Habit*, Charles Duhigg writes, "We know that a habit cannot be eradicated—it must, instead, be replaced... The evidence is clear: If you want to change a habit, you must find an alternative routine and your odds of success go up dramatically when you commit to changing as part of a group."[2] The framework he gives in the book for reshaping habits is as follows:

- Identify the routine.
- Experiment with rewards.
- Isolate the cue.
- Have a plan.

Taking time to understand your habits and to replace the ones that have not been serving you well is an important part of the growth process. You can change, and the experiences that come from those changes will be powerful demonstrations of a life that has risen.

DIGITAL DETOX

When I went to my therapy intensive at Onsite, I had to give up my phone for six days. It was the thing I was most nervous about. It wasn't leaving my kids and not talking to them that scared me (I knew they would be fine). It wasn't leaving my work and not working at all for an extended period (something I haven't done once in my adult life). It wasn't dealing with trauma from my past (I knew I signed up for that).

It was not. having. my. phone.

They say you pick up your phone 144 times a day,[3] and if I am honest, I probably pick mine up more. My job is primarily social media, and if I am not on it, I am scrolling, filming, editing on my phone. I really didn't know how I would do it. How would it change me? What would I learn about myself and others?

The first days were really hard. I found myself reaching for my phone, only to grasp air. I missed connecting with other people—texting and phone calls and social media. I missed documenting my day through photos and videos. But also, I found myself really present in my circumstances, maybe more than I had been in decades. All I had were the people in front of me, the outdoors around me, and myself. Over the course of the intensive, I spent roughly a hundred hours connected to these things instead of technology. It was unfamiliar to have all that space for connection only. But it was really, really good.

While I was the first person to happily get my phone back, I must say that I really enjoyed the exercise of disconnecting. Interestingly, I realized the next day that during my time at Onsite, I thought a lot less about my body because I was not comparing it all day every day to bodies I was seeing on social media. I also reflected on ways I used social media for validation personally and professionally.

The average American spends four to five hours a day looking at a phone. Consider your attachment to your phone. Are you missing out on experiences because you are too connected to your device? Do you maybe pick up your phone and zone out instead of really connecting with others and/or yourself? Some strategies for disconnecting with your devices include:

- **Set screen limits.** You can set your device to shut down certain apps so that you limit their usage.
- **Put your phone somewhere else.** Sometimes all it takes is putting your phone in a different room so that it eliminates the temptation to constantly pick it up and mindlessly scroll.
- **Take breaks.** Set times of day or even entire days when you are not connected to your phone.
- **Turn off notifications.** Every ping is a calling for you to pick up your phone. Turn off notifications to reduce distractions.
- **Get accountability from a friend.** Ask a friend to hold you accountable about how much you are using your phone.
- **Set boundaries.** Create rules for when you can and can't use your phone, such as no phones at the table or in bed.

Much research has been done around our digital habits and the ways they contribute (positively and negatively) to our experiences. Paying attention to the way you are using devices, social media, and so on, and considering the shifts you may need to make will positively affect your experiences. I'll never forget when I had a group of my son's friends over. They were all in eighth grade, and everyone had a phone at the table. I collected all of their phones so they could enjoy dinner together without the distraction of a device. They didn't really complain, though a few eye rolls were exchanged. But what ensued was more laughter, more fun, and more presence. Consider how your own device habits may be diminishing your day-to-day experiences and preventing you from really engaging with your life.

CREATE AN EXPERIENCE BUCKET LIST

About ten years ago, I started creating seasonal bucket lists with my family. We typically create a summer bucket list and a holiday bucket list. For instance, in summer the list might include go to the water park, take a vacation, go get ice cream, and so on. At the holidays, it usually includes watch *Elf,* go see Christmas lights, make sugar cookies. These lists provide a guide for our activities during these busy seasons. We like to think of the bucket lists as our must-do activities. The things on the list are the activities that will make our season great. Then, anything else we do is like icing on the cake.

Simply by writing down our bucket list, we are taking ownership of the way we spend our time. We are making it a priority to hear what is most important to everyone in the family. It is also a bonding experience to create the list as a family.

This practice has caused me to want to get more specific with my life bucket lists. I will say things like, "Oh, visiting Australia is on my bucket list." But the truth is, for a long time, I didn't have a bucket list. These sentiments were longings I would share without codifying them in any way.

One day, I started a Google Doc titled "Bucket Lists." On it, I created bucket categories that made sense for me:

- Work bucket list
- Travel bucket list
- Family bucket list
- Personal bucket list

By writing down my bucket list experiences in each of these categories, I had a tangible list to reflect on for how to spend my time. It also oriented me toward the future. Creating a bucket list says, *I am more focused on where I am going instead of where I have been.* It is an excellent exercise as you shape your life into what you want it to be. You get to create your future experiences, and a bucket list is an excellent way to help shape what those will be.

Also, bucket lists are not set in stone. They get to evolve and change as time goes on. The benefit is in writing down what matters to you. What are your goals and dreams for the different areas of your life? What do you hope to experience and accomplish? Simply by taking the time to write these things down, you are making them a priority.

YOU HAVE ONE LIFE

After my divorce, my awareness of experiences heightened. So many things felt new, different, and unfamiliar. For instance, I traveled with one boyfriend every four weeks or so because of his work. We went on adventures together, just the two of us. It was fun and exciting and so different from my previous life experiences.

Of course, most of my new experiences weren't fun travel experiences. They were things like navigating taxes for the first time by myself (with the help of an accountant) and tackling home projects on my own. No matter what the experience, the result was the same: a stretching of myself, my abilities, and my perspective. I found great joy in the rebuilding process. I truly fell more in love with my life.

And I think the same will happen for you. Experiences create wonder, confidence, and competence. During this season of growth, you are going to learn and experience a lot. With those new experiences will come much fruit.

Embrace your new experiences as positive things in your life—even if they are hard, nerve-racking, or simply unfamiliar. You have one life, and it is the things you do that make it vibrant and beautiful. So whether it is like my confidence-building experiences in dating or my letting go of traditions like going to a concert, I can honestly say that the new experiences in this season have shaped me in so many positive ways. I know that the same will be true for you.

CHAPTER 11

MAKING TIME FOR
CREATIVE PURSUITS

While vacationing in Destin, Florida, a few years ago, we discovered a place called the Shard Shop. The Shard Shop was founded by an artist named Mary Hong, who creates the most astonishing art out of shards of glass. The shards of glass are assembled into beautiful and creative designs. Resin is then poured over the glass to seal everything into place. Her finished works are one-of-a-kind masterpieces. I wish I could take you to see Mary's work. Each one is creative and astonishingly beautiful.

Guests of the Shard Shop can create their own pieces out of broken glass, similar to the art that Mary makes (though less intricate). It is a creative experience unlike any other, and it has become one of my favorite things to do when we vacation in Destin. Our family has gone multiple times, and we always enjoy the process of creating something special out of shards of glass.

The shop has large bins lining one wall, each bin filled with a different color of broken glass—pinks, blues, greens, whites, oranges, and more. Sometimes you can tell when the glass was once a part of a bottle, a vase, a wine flute, or something else.

Patrons use cups to carefully gather glass to use in their own projects. Then, the work begins of creating art using the broken pieces.

The process is slow and methodical, but when broken pieces of glass are assembled with other broken pieces, you create something that is unique and one of a kind.

I have been working on a tree series over the years. The first time I went to the Shard Shop, I made a tree in spring. Pink glass dotted the tree's branches, representing new life.

The next time, I made a tree in winter, covered in clear and white glass, heavy with snow and ice.

Last time I went, I made a tree in summer, green and lush with life. I used green bottle shards for the leaves.

I think the Shard Shop is an analogy for life. We have the opportunity to create a beautiful life, though it might mean we are assembling broken pieces to make something new. When we are meticulous and diligent to do the work with intention and care, we will be met with something more beautiful than before.

I also believe that we must carve out time to be creative in our daily lives. Creative practices allow us to try new things, stretch our minds, slow our thinking, and allow space for art to emerge. It is sacred, nuanced, and life-giving to be creative. In my life, I have found that if I go too long without being creative, I am grumpier. No matter how busy, overwhelmed, or stressed I am, enjoying creative practices and my passions pays so many positive dividends. Creativity always makes things better, not worse.

FIND TIME TO BE CREATIVE

As you are healing from a disappointment, making time for creativity is one of the best activities you can pursue. Creativity allows us to stretch muscles that we don't typically use, stimulating parts of our brain that might be dormant. Those creative muscles need to be attended to. But this can feel daunting.

During periods of intense disappointment or transition, it might be really difficult to feel like you should make creativity a priority. But what I know to be true is that when you make time for creativity, your life expands, not contracts. We all need to explore creative pursuits to help us thrive in the world. Those creative pursuits will be varied based on your interests and abilities. They might be cooking, baking, painting, writing, drawing, woodworking, embroidery, or something else. The point is that you will be made better for doing these types of things.

When I was a little girl, I loved to paint. I think this was because my mom was a hobby artist, and she loved to paint. And so I would often sit down with a brush and some watercolors or acrylic paint and create something from nothing. Now that I'm a parent, I can imagine that my mom encouraged me to pursue those creative endeavors because they were really helpful in regulating emotions and helping me relax in my world. Now, as an adult, I need to use those same creative muscles for the same reasons.

In my first book, *The Fringe Hours: Making Time for You*, I share steps on how to make time for creative practices. One of the most foundational principles in that book is that I ask readers to track their time for a week. This exercise is an effective way to look at how you spend time through a fresh perspective. Write down everything you do, not just the big stuff. After a week of documenting, evaluate the following:

- What are the need-to-dos that you cannot eliminate, such as school and work?
- What are the nice-to-dos? This is everything that is not required. Even cooking dinner is a nice-to-do, because you could order out.

- Is there anything that you said yes to because you thought you should, not because you wanted to? Can you cut that thing?
- Where are opportunities to reclaim your time?

Interestingly, as I have traveled around the country for the past ten years talking about that book and self-care, one of the common pieces of feedback I hear from women is that they don't have time for themselves and their creative pursuits. This exercise shows them that they usually do have time; they just are investing their time in other things.

WHAT DO YOU LOVE TO DO?

Once you identify where you can find the time, the next step is doing the thing you love—reading, writing, going outside, planting a garden, painting, and so on. But some people don't even know what they would do if they had the time. So many women fill their time with the other people and responsibilities of their life that pursuing their own creative endeavors is something that has long been forgotten. Add in a major disappointment, and you might further feel like creativity is the last thing you should be spending your time on. The very idea of free time to pursue something creative seems ludicrous and inaccessible.

I'll never forget a conference I spoke at a few years ago. I asked women in the room to raise their hands and share when the last time was that they lost track of time doing something they love. One woman who appeared to be in her mid- to late forties raised her hand and said that it was when her last child was born. I asked how old the child was, thinking that surely the child was a baby, and she told me that the child was in fact a teenager. Yes, it had been fifteen years since she had last lost track of time doing something she loved.

Do either of the two following scenarios ring true to you? Do you ever think to yourself:

I don't have time to _____ because I need to keep house, go to work, run my kids to their activities, do chores, and so on? There simply are not enough hours in a day. Any hobbies should continue to take a back seat to my responsibilities. You don't know what my life is like.

Even if I did have time for myself, what would I actually do? I wouldn't know where to begin. Plus, my time would probably be better spent tackling my to-do list.

Breaking out of your routines to do something creative will enable you to shift your focus and create a sense of peace in your day. Yes, it might feel unfamiliar and difficult at first, but the more you do it, the easier it will become.

After you have identified what time you have available and what creative passion you would like to do, now you have to do it. Where you spend your time points to what you value. Make spending this time on something creative and life-giving a priority. Over the course of my life, I have discovered, again and again, that in seasons when I don't have creative experiences, I am not my best self. This is because I am not properly filling my cup and nurturing my creative side.

HOW TO FIND CREATIVE ENDEAVORS

Discovering creative hobbies can be a fun but sometimes daunting endeavor. How do you know what you will like and won't like? Where do you begin?

In January 2020, I took an embroidery class at a local sewing shop. I had never stitched before, except for a brief period of time in my childhood where I cross-stitched tiny samplers. But I remembered that nine-year-old Jessica really loved stitching those samplers and thought I would enjoy embroidery. So I asked Matthew if he would buy a class for me for Christmas. It seemed like the perfect gift. He did and so I had no choice but to learn. The class seemed low risk as far as trying new hobbies goes, as it was just a few hours, included all the supplies, and was not far from my house.

Well, that few hours changed my life, though I didn't realize it then. I immediately loved the slowness of stitching tiny shapes and flowers. I loved learning the variety of stitches. And I loved the peace my body had as I stitched.

Little did I know that two months later, the world would shut down and that new hobby would become a life-giving constant in my life. I discovered embroidery-focused social media accounts and started taking online classes with a teacher in England. She made stitching fun and accessible and soon I was stitching nearly every day.

During a season when everything felt tumultuous—in my marriage, my work, and literally the world—the creative practice of embroidery saved me. It gave me something positive to invest my time in. It was calming and I was so proud of every sampler I created. Today they all hang in my home, serving as reminders of a season that was hard, but I still took care of myself. I truly believe that creativity serves all of us well.

Here are some simple practices that can help you discover a creative hobby that you love:

- **Consider your childhood interests.** What did you like to do as a kid? Just because you are older doesn't mean you wouldn't like the same thing now.
- **Sign up for an online craft class portal.** Sites like Creativebug and Craftsy offer thousands of instructional

videos on a variety of hobbies. These sites can give you access to great teachers and experts in their fields and diverse options for creative pursuits. You will have the freedom to learn a lot for a very affordable price. Plus, because the instruction is via video, you can learn at your own pace.

- **Go to the library.** You can learn how to do just about anything through a book. Find a topic that interests you and check out a few how-to books.
- **Consider your media habits.** Do you tend to watch a lot of cooking or craft shows? What do you like to save on Pinterest or Instagram? These might be indicators of hobbies that you might enjoy.
- **Think about who inspires you.** Is there someone who inspires you by their creativity or a hobby that they enjoy? For instance, my friend Mallory loves to make sourdough and shares about it on her Instagram. She has inspired so many other people to try the art of breadmaking simply by witnessing her passion.

START WRITING

Have you ever journaled as a form of creative expression? The act of documenting the ordinary and extraordinary can be a healing practice. Many people find that journaling allows them to put things on the page that they find hard to articulate verbally. Some of the benefits of journaling include:

- Reducing anxiety
- Breaking away from the nonstop cycle of obsessive thinking and brooding

- Improving the perception of events
- Regulating emotions
- Encouraging awareness
- Boosting physical health

Journaling can be done in many forms, including written on a page, drawn, or typed. Some people like the process of using pen and paper, while others appreciate the ease of using a device. If you have never journaled before or the idea feels daunting, consider this list of possible journals you could create:

- **Stream-of-Consciousness Journaling.** This type of journaling is just like it sounds: you simply write. You don't have parameters to follow when you write whatever comes into your head.
- **Art Journaling.** In this type of journal, you use collage, paint, markers, and pencils to explore your feelings, moods, and experiences. The joy is in the creative process.
- **Bullet Journaling.** In bullet journaling, you focus on making bulleted lists. These lists can be as detailed or as simple as you would like.
- **Photo Journaling.** Take a photo every day and write about that memory or experience. The photo is the prompt to write about your everyday. As a former scrapbooker, I used to document in this way. I love that it caused me to document stories and images that I otherwise wouldn't have.
- **Letter Journaling.** In letter journaling, you write letters either to yourself or to other people that you will never send. These letters are a way of releasing and processing experiences and feelings.

- **Morning Pages Journaling.** This form of journaling was made popular by Julia Cameron's book *The Artist's Way*.[1] Morning pages is a stream-of-consciousness journaling exercise that is done first thing in the morning. You write three pages about anything and everything, and then you stop.

TAKE A CREATIVE CLASS

Last year, I took a pottery class. I think since seeing *Ghost* as a kid (by the way, this is *not* a kids' movie), I have been intrigued by the idea of throwing clay on a wheel and turning nothing into something beautiful. I thought it would be easy, but pottery is much more difficult than I thought it would be. It requires way more precision, patience, and slowness than I ever imagined. Demi and Patrick made it look so simple.

The class was six weeks long, and we started with the basics. Each week, we learned new techniques and formed different objects. Bowls, vases, mugs—we made them all. What I didn't realize is that pottery requires so much more than just throwing clay on the wheel and moving your hands in a motion that forms a bowl or vase. To get the right shape, you must use firm pressure, but not too much or the form will not be right. You also do a lot of shaving and cutting away with special tools. Precision matters in pottery. You weigh the clay to get the right size piece and then fine-tune throughout the formation process.

Honestly, I was the worst student in the class. It was supposed to be a beginner class, but some of the people were definitely not beginners. One woman had watched YouTube videos during the pandemic and bought a wheel for her house on Amazon. Another woman had done pottery classes in high school. Still another was doing private lessons in addition to these. As for me? I literally bought the starter pack at the counter before the class and had never watched anything about pottery besides rom-com movies.

My newness and lack of skill showed. Everyone would be running their wheels and doing great, and then there was me. I would use too much force and my bowl would be lopsided. I'd push too hard and my vase would collapse. My clay wasn't centered or would get air pockets. I was kind of a disaster as I struggled to get the right rhythms. But I didn't give up. Instead, I asked for a lot of help. I wasn't ashamed. I was there to learn, and learn I would! My teacher would come to my wheel and demonstrate the motions. Sometimes she would use her hands with mine to ensure I didn't fail. She never criticized or made me feel less than. Instead her steadiness steadied me.

As the weeks went on, I got more comfortable with the process. I loved the feel of the clay and the process of making something new. Not every bowl was a failure. I made a mug that would hold a small cup of tea. One week I formed a small vase. My pieces slowly stacked up week after week. I was excited when it was time to glaze our items, after a month of creating them. In pottery, the glaze looks nothing like what the finished piece will look like. The colors are muted and far from the vibrant shades that emerge from the firing process. I considered the finished color samples and dipped my pieces, excited for what they would look like the next week.

Our pieces were fired and finished for our final week of class. I was so excited to go. As I walked in and went over to the shelf marked "Jessica," there were my pieces, shining in black, green, and white. I didn't see the imperfections like I thought I would. I saw hard work and effort. I saw beauty and uniqueness. I saw art. And I was so proud of how far I had come. I made those. And they were stunning.

Pottery is a lot like life. You have to work to form the life you want. There is pushing and pulling that happens. Things have to be cut away. And beauty often emerges from fire, just like a finished pot is finally completed after it has been fired. Your heart needs some creativity as you work through your own story. Consider trying something new or old and letting yourself get lost in the time to do it. It will be a healing balm on the wounds of your journey.

CHAPTER 12

EMBRACING SPIRITUAL PRACTICES

As someone who is a practicing Christian, I found that my faith played a huge role in helping me as I navigated the pain of my divorce and the healing afterward. This chapter is intended to serve as a small guide to some practices that were helpful for me and may be helpful for you. I am not a spiritual teacher, and this chapter is far from exhaustive, but I hope it will be useful if you are someone who believes in God. Of course, please feel free to skip ahead if it does not resonate with you.

Why does God allow bad things to happen to good people?

If God loves me, why am I going through this?

Why isn't God answering my prayers?

God, I thought it would be better than this.

The Bible is full of suffering and longing. In fact, the only guarantee about life is that at some point we will be disappointed. During Holy Week, which is the week before Easter, we read of Jesus being celebrated as he rode through the city on a donkey, flipping tables in the temple, feasting at the Last Supper, being betrayed by one of his closest friends, dying on the cross, and rising from the dead three days later. Holy Week feels a lot like life, where one minute everything is wonderful and you're celebrating, and in the blink of an eye everything shatters. Jesus could not avoid suffering, and neither can we.

The road I walked as my marriage unraveled and I began again was one marked by painful points. It was my own Gethsemane Road.

I think about Jesus praying in the garden before he was arrested, asking God if there was another way. He prayed, "Father, if you are willing, take this cup from me; yet not my will, but yours be done" (Luke 22:42). He, too, yearned for a different story. Maybe you can relate?

So often I have prayed that first part of Jesus' prayer: *Take this away from me. I don't want this. Please.* For instance, when Matthew and I were still married but trying to decide what steps to take after he came out, I remember so many nights when I would just lie in bed and pray: *Lord, please bring him back to me,* meaning, *Bring back the man I married, the man who wanted me, the man for whom I was enough.* I wanted the life I imagined and the man that I knew (or thought I knew). Of course, you know how the story goes. God did not bring him back. At least, not in the way I wanted.

Months after Matthew moved out, I was in bed alone, in my house alone. I remember thinking about Matthew and then feeling the presence of God clearly speaking to my heart, saying, *I brought him back.* It was an aha gift from God. In coming out, Matthew did come back to me. He was more vibrant and more connected to the kids and seemed more present than he had been in years. He was back. It was not the back I had prayed for, but it was still an answer.

I never prayed for God's will to be done, believing that bringing Matthew back was the best option. I wanted my husband. I wanted my family intact. I didn't want to start over. I thought I knew more than God. It turned out that for me, for Matthew, and for our kids, God's will was different. This is true so often in life. We think we know what we want and need. We pray for those specific things. And then life doesn't go that way. But that doesn't mean that God isn't kind. Sometimes His kindness looks different from how we think it should or will.

REMEMBER YOU'RE NOT ALONE

A work colleague texted me after the news had come out about Matthew and my divorce. "I was listening to this song this morning, and I felt prompted to share it with you." The song was "The Blessing," sung by Elevation Worship, Kari Jobe, and Cody Carnes, which I had never heard before. I asked Alexa to play it and was immediately taken by the simple lyrics. The song opens with the Bible verses Numbers 6:24–26, which says, "The Lord bless you and keep you; the Lord make his face shine on you and be gracious to you; the Lord turn his face toward you and give you peace." It then goes on to proclaim a prayer asking for the Lord to be with us and the generations that come after us. It ministered to me on lonely days when I felt alone to know that God was always with me.

Even though I felt so alone in my despair, the idea that I actually wasn't brought me much comfort during that time. I would listen to that song on repeat, usually in my kitchen, cooking, cleaning, crying, and begging for those words to be true.

Believing that God was with me helped me during the moments when I felt most alone. I would pray and sing, asking for God to hold me, guide me, and give me wisdom as I navigated these uncharted waters.

So much scripture in the Bible speaks of God being with us. If you feel alone in your journey, take comfort that you are not. You are known, held, and loved by God.

TRUST IN THE SLOW WORK OF GOD

Several years after my marriage ended, I remember being frustrated that things were not going better from a dating perspective. I knew I was a good partner and that I wanted to love again, but I kept being met with heartbreak. When I was processing with a friend, she shared a line from a letter written by Pierre Teilhard de Chardin, which says, "Above all, trust in the slow work of God. We are quite naturally impatient in everything to reach the end without delay."[1] Ah yes, that was something I could sit with and understand. The previous few years had been wildly slow. And yet, God. I could see how He took what could have been awful and turned it for good. I saw His work in my life and in the lives of those I loved. But I could not have imagined any of it when I was in the midst of my turmoil.

We can become very impatient when we are in crisis or grief. We want a resolution now. We don't want to wait. And sometimes things seem so dark that we don't even know that we can wait for something. Like when Jesus was buried in the tomb, no one could have imagined that He would rise. It was simply darkness, grief, and despair.

But the slowness of God is always at work. Time and again in my life I have seen this play out, and goodness came, even if it was different from what I expected. Sometimes, we can see the way that God was working for our good, but sometimes we can't. Either way, I believe that eventually, we can see the big picture and understand how things happened the way they should have. Like my friend said, we must trust in the slowness of God.

ASK FOR PRAYER

"Will you please light a candle for me?"

It was a simple but vulnerable text to my friend Mallory on a hard day (she's also my sourdough friend!). I saw her post on Instagram that she was lighting candles and lifting up prayers for people in her community, and I reached out. Mallory is a prayer warrior and has a beautiful candle stand in her home, just like those you see in Catholic churches around the world. In it are fifty votive cups, and she lights candles and offers prayers to God and presence to those in her life.

She replied that she would light one for me and reminded me I wasn't alone. She also thanked me for letting her pray for me. Sometimes we might feel like we are being a burden by asking for prayer, but I have never had someone say anything close to that. In fact, I think most people are like Mallory and honored to pray for the people they love. I think asking for prayer is powerful because it invites others into our story and shows that we believe something greater than ourselves is at work. And when we are struggling, those two things—community and faith—lead to strength.

I once visited a church, and right in the middle of the service, the pastor invited people to share prayer requests. People started raising their hands and said things like:

- Pray for my mom, who is at the hospital undergoing tests for an unknown illness.
- Pray for my husband, who is celebrating one year of sobriety.
- Pray for me as I pursue my graduate degree.
- Pray for my daughter, who is traveling.

The pastor stood at the pulpit with a journal and wrote down every name and petition. I thought it was such a picture of God and the way He longs to hear from us. I also thought it was sacred that people would boldly proclaim their prayers to their congregation. It was a reminder that I think many people want to be known and have their petitions lifted up.

I'll never forget the first time I walked into a clothing store outside of Nashville and saw a visual representation of people yearning for prayer. I know it sounds unusual, but let me tell you about it.

This store, which is called Philanthropy, is in this quaint downtown just south of Nashville, which is filled with charming small businesses. Philanthropy is decorated with antiques and boho decor. Most of the store is stocked with beautiful clothes, along with a small selection of gifts and books. In the center of this store is what looks like a small greenhouse. This is the prayer room. Inside those four walls within that boutique are hundreds and hundreds of tags where people have recorded prayer requests. Hooks line the room, and on each hook are many tags, dangling in hope. Some of the tags have names. Some say things like "my mom" or "my dad." Others have requests for healing, for work, for relief. All of them point to hopes, dreams, disappointments, and pain. Whenever I go to that store, I love that spot. It seems wild to me that such a sacred, vulnerable spot could exist in a seemingly normal clothing store, but there it is.

And isn't that reminiscent of life? In the middle of something that looks normal probably exists a yearning, a pain, a prayer for life to be better than this. And along with that prayer are people you know and people you don't who will be willing to pray for you. You just have to be brave enough to ask.

BLESS YOUR ACTUAL DAYS

The practice of blessing your life as it is right now is one I have become more attuned to thanks to the writing of Kate Bowler and Jessica Richie. In their book, *The Lives We Actually Have: 100*

Blessings for Imperfect Days, they explain that blessings are for everyday moments, both good and bad. They write:

> The act of blessing is the strange and vital work of noticing what is true about God and ourselves…But in the act of blessing the world as it is and as it should be, we are starting to reassemble what we know. Maybe, God, you are here in the midst of this grief. Maybe, God, you can provide for this specific problem…When I bless the actual days I am living, I suddenly find I have a great deal more to say that is honest. I am mourning. I am bored. I am exhausted. I am apathetic…Good or bad, I don't have to wait to say something spiritually true. I can simply bless it all instead.[2]

I love the idea of blessing the day, the moment, the experience you are in. God does not require perfection or curation. We are created and welcomed in just as we are. So, as you go about your healing and growing, what can you bless? I have written one blessing below. These are honest words for a hard day.

A BLESSING FOR HARD DAYS

God, everything feels hard right now.
Bless my heart, which feels fragile and tender.
Bless my home, which is full of chaos and mess,
    but also love for my kids and myself.
Bless my body, which feels weary and stressed.

May I know that you are with me, even when I
    feel alone and sad.
Will you show me a glimmer of your presence?

I am tired of hoping.
I am desperate for something new and better.

Bless me where I am today and give me the energy
     to keep going.
I know that better days are ahead, but today is not
     a better day. Today is a hard day.
Be with me in it.

Below I have provided space for you to write your own blessing.

_____

_____

_____

_____

_____

_____

_____

_____

MEDITATE

I have never been one to slow down. Practices like yoga and meditation have always been difficult for me. My mind tends to continuously be spinning, thinking about the next thing. Stillness and quieting have been so hard that I have chosen to ignore their benefits.

In recent years, I have adopted practices of meditation and seen its benefits. I asked counselor Christopher O'Reilly about meditation, and he shared with me, "Meditation can be a foundational practice that can be extremely helpful to developing and maintaining emotional and physical health. There is a stress or strain when our thoughts are in a different space than our bodies, which happens frequently. When we practice meditation, we are bringing our thoughts and attention into the same time and space as our bodies, which is the present moment. Our bodies are always in the present moment, which is why they are often a focal point for the meditation practice."

Meditation is another spiritual practice that can be grounding in all seasons of life—from the most stressful and disappointing to times of growth and healing. Anyone can meditate. It is something that requires nothing more than an open heart and willingness to try it. If you are interested in meditation, you can find numerous free resources on the internet, including YouTube, and many meditation apps. I especially like the meditation practices offered on Peloton and Headspace.

GO OUTSIDE

When my friend Ann's dad unexpectedly passed away, I coordinated a group gift from a bunch of her friends to give her a kayak. She has a pond on her farm that she would often go to for a bit of solitude and prayer, and I knew that the kayak would provide comfort during that season. I'll never forget the way that gift ministered to her. She said it felt like the boat was her friends holding her in her grief as she mourned and prayed, surrounded by the sounds of the wind, water, and birds.

Nature is a way that many people connect to their spirituality. When we are outside we sense our smallness in the world. It becomes easier to connect to the Creator when we are in His creation.

Some simple ways to incorporate being outside into your faith practices:

- Go outside to pray.
- Start your day outside.
- Go for a prayer walk.
- Spend time gardening.
- Explore and look for little wonders.
- Lie in the grass and connect with the physicality of the earth on your back.

PRACTICE GRATITUDE

When everything feels out of whack and you are looking for something to grab hold of, starting a gratitude practice can be the life-giving and life-saving tool you need. Practicing gratitude shifts our perspective to all the goodness of our life, but this is just the beginning. Research shows that "from childhood to old age, a wide array of psychological, physical, and relational benefits are associated with gratitude. Gratitude has been shown to contribute not only to an increase in happiness, health, and other desirable life outcomes but also to a decrease in negative affect and problematic functioning."[3]

One of the benefits I have seen with practicing gratitude is an increased awareness of the big and small positive things in life. On my gratitude lists over the years, I have written so many simple things, like:

I'm grateful that today was sunny.

I'm grateful for comfortable shoes.

I'm grateful for the kindness of the lady at the grocery store.

Gratitude expands your perspective and opens your eyes to the goodness in your world. Because even when things are crashing down, there is still goodness to embrace. Even when I would drive to work, crying nearly every day, I was grateful for things in my life. I was grateful for coworkers who felt like family, for my kids and their daily joy, for the sun on my face, for my health, and more. Clinging to these things helped to get me through my hard time.

Many gratitude journals exist, though a simple plain notebook or even your notetaking app works just as well. Try writing down three good things every day before you go to bed. One study on this practice found that people who did this practice had increased levels of happiness and positive well-being, even months after the study was completed.[4] The point is, look for things to be thankful for every day, and then take it a step further and write it down.

YOU WILL RISE

When we think about the Easter story, we remember that it doesn't end with the crucifixion. The best part of the story—the reason we celebrate Easter—is the empty tomb, the resurrection. I believe deeply that we all have a resurrection story in our lives. We all have disappointments that feel like death, and ultimately we have a choice. Will we bury the thing that died, or will we rise after the burial?

Throughout the past few years, my faith has brought me much comfort. I have been reminded that even when I feel lonely, I am not alone, that I can trust in the slow work of God and that others can pray for me on my behalf. Faith is belief in the things unseen, and from mysteries of God to the mysteries of my own life, it is that faith that has carried me. My faith has brought me the promise and confidence that resurrection is possible.

CHAPTER 13

ACCEPTING WHAT IS AND WILL BE

I love peonies. Are you familiar with them? Peonies are flowers that grow on bushes and bloom big, glorious blooms in the spring. I wait all year for them to bloom, and those weeks in May are some of my happiest in my yard. The flowers are huge, gorgeous, and jaw-dropping.

Do you know what makes a peony thrive? Cold. Yep, peonies need winter to bloom. The best time to plant them is actually in the fall and winter because they need the cold months to really take root. If you plant them in the spring, they won't flourish like they would if they are planted in the cooler months. You see where I am going here, don't you? The most beautiful flowers in my garden only get that beautiful when they go through a dark, cold winter.

It's late February right now when I am writing this, and I just stepped outside to look at where my peony bushes grow. You know what I saw? The tiniest purple shoots springing from the ground. My peony bushes are sprouting. And soon, their glory will abound for all to enjoy. I cannot wait.

Those peony bushes are a reflection of what I have seen in my own story. I have experienced the greatest beauty and growth after the hardest of times. The winter of your disappointment will birth a spring of beauty. Winter doesn't last forever. It simply can't. Spring must come.

It's hard to remember that on those cold, lonely winter days of disappointment and sorrow. My divorce was finalized on the winter equinox, just a few days before Christmas. I remember the pit in my stomach as I pulled the signed, stamped papers out of a manila envelope. There it was. A sixteen-year marriage, over. I looked at the judge's signature and wondered how many divorce decrees he had signed, representing so much sorrow and ache for each different story. I wondered if he realized that his signature marked a winter.

That night, my daughter and I went to a concert at the Nashville Symphony. It was the Drew and Ellie Holcomb Christmas show. The husband-and-wife duo are magic on stage, both together and individually. About halfway through the show, Ellie sang her song "Constellations." If you have never heard it, stop reading and pull it up on your favorite music app. It's a song of longing, loneliness, pain, and beauty at the same time. Tears silently slipped down my face as she cried out to God in her lyrics, singing:

> 'Cause out here in the dark
> Underneath a canopy of stars
> Constellations falling from Your heart
> They tell me that I'm not alone

I felt alone in that moment, in the dark of the symphony hall and the dark sorrow of my heart. The thing about winter is that spring always comes, but you must get through the coldest, darkest days first. Days that feel lonely and relentless. They are long, dark, and cold. But all of a sudden, it's light after five o'clock. The weather shifts. The ground softens, and gardens begin to sprout. What once was brown and barren becomes lush and green.

This is true in life as well. I realize this isn't a new analogy, but I found it to be so profoundly accurate during my season of deep turmoil. For a long time everything felt dark, cold, and lonely. It was difficult to accept that this was my new normal. But slowly, I accepted things and then began to thrive.

MESSY HOPE

On a hard day, a friend reached out to me and said, "I see you in this place of messy hope." I latched on to that phrase because it was such an accurate way to describe the hope that I felt. So many people talk about hope in a sort of perfect, angelic way, like the quote that hope is something with feathers. Sometimes, sure. But other times, hope is much less tidy and charming than an angel or a bird.

In 2022, Nashville had a cold freeze that killed thousands of plants, bushes, and trees. On my property I had five boxwoods, which are these gorgeous bushes that provided both privacy and beauty. They were likely twenty to thirty years old. We had plenty of snows and cold weather and they were always fine, but not that winter. They all died.

For a long time I held on to hope that they would come back. I waited for new shoots to grow. I held on to hope that they weren't really dead. But they were. Finally I made the tough choice to have those bushes cut down and ripped out from the earth.

Immediately I noticed how much better the space looked without them there. The barren, dead wood was replaced by space and light in my yard. For two years, I had hung on to hope for something that was dead. Once I let go and moved forward with the obvious right choice—removing the dead bushes—I experienced new light in my yard.

Similarly, in life, hope is messy. We sometimes have a hard time letting go of things, even when they are clearly dead, because it is all we know. We can't imagine another way. I couldn't imagine my yard without those big bushes there—so much so that I wanted to leave their dead sticks there in place of the green that had once been.

When you start to emerge from the depths of grief, sometimes it can feel like you are just waiting for the other shoe to drop. You become fearful that something else is going to happen. Hope can also be exhausting. The waiting. The wondering. The anticipation of things that sometimes don't ever come.

COMPARISON

I recently joined a gym, but not just any gym. A boot camp gym. The kind of gym where it seems like everyone is a badass. During my second class, I thought I might die. I couldn't breathe for most of the forty-five-minute class. At one point, our circuit included jumping over small hurdles. The instructor said if we needed to modify, we could just jump over the line in the room. Since I have never jumped in my life except if I was startled in a movie, I thought the line was sufficient. But after a few jumps, the trainer came over and placed a hurdle in front of me. Apparently she believed that I could jump over it. She was the only one. But I figured if she believed, maybe I should, too. It was yellow and twelve inches tall. I looked at it for a minute and then hopped over it haphazardly, with one foot following the other instead of both in the air at the same time.

I looked at her and said, "I'm not sure I am doing this right." She said, "Use your power and jump with both feet at once." I took a breath, bent slightly, and jumped. I got over it with ease. After a few more jumps, I was successfully hopping like the other women in the room. I felt strong and powerful. Then I looked up and saw my new friend to my right hopping over huge hurdles. Instead of my meager twelve inches, these hurdles were twenty-eight inches high. She took a breath and jumped so high she cleared the hurdle with inches to spare. I was incredulous. Immediately I went from feeling strong to feeling pathetic and weak. My twelve inches was now a disappointment instead of a feat. I did my best to stay focused on my hurdle, but her jumps in my periphery kept reminding me how far I had to go. Instead of being proud of my beginning, I was comparing myself to someone else's middle.

Comparison is like that, isn't it? We can go from high to low in an instant. Sometimes we will compare grief stories and disappointments. I have joked to people, "My COVID lockdown was worse than yours. My husband came out." But honestly, that isn't funny or true. There isn't a worse whatever. Our sorrow is our sorrow. Our triumph is our triumph. Me jumping twelve inches was as amazing as my new friend jumping twenty-eight inches. We cannot get caught up in looking at what other people are doing and comparing to what we are working on, going through, and achieving. Instead we must solely focus on our work. What do we need to do to keep getting stronger, growing, and, in the case of my gym example, jumping higher? Those are things we must focus on.

Have you ever seen a horse pulling a buggy or racing while wearing blinders over his eyes? These blinders are used to reduce the horse's vision so that he doesn't get spooked by what he is pulling or what is alongside him. It keeps his focus on the path ahead and the job he is doing. Sometimes I need metaphorical blinders to ensure I also keep my focus on what it is ahead, instead of what is to my left or right. These ensure that comparison is not a thief of our joy and the good, hard work we are doing.

Instead of comparing yourself, your story, your suffering, focus only on what is before you and on moving forward. Have compassion for yourself and where you are instead of comparing yourself to where others are. Because when you have compassion, you will be gentler, slower, and kinder toward yourself and your circumstances. This isn't always easy, but it is worth pursuing that compassion. You deserve it and need it, especially when the days are long as you heal and rebuild.

GRACE FOR OUR YOUNGER SELVES

As we become further and further removed from our situation, sometimes we will look back at our former selves and question the choices we made or the knowledge we had or didn't have. One of the hardest parts of my story was how I couldn't have known. Why did I not connect the dots? Why did I not see that my husband, whom I loved deeply and thought I knew better than myself, was gay?

I used to be a big scrapbooker. I have albums and albums full of photos, words, stickers, and memories. I've looked at some of those albums recently and I've been drawn to the youth and innocence of myself in those early years. I have come to realize that we must have grace and compassion for our former selves. Me not knowing that Matthew was gay did not mean I was dumb or blind for not realizing it. I did the best with the information that I had. Likewise, you likely have made the best decisions with the information and life you have. It is so important to not look back on ourselves with judgment or frustration.

One of the greatest gifts of life is that we continue to learn, evolve, and grow. The opposite of growth is death, and if you are here reading this book, then you are fighting for growth and life.

When I went to Onsite, we did an exercise where we walked a labyrinth, and we thought about our stories while we walked. It was early morning, and the air was already damp and buggy. A leader guided us through a meditation and gave us a bit of anchoring for the exercise, and then he spurred us to walk this path. At that moment, in the distance a man played bagpipes, which added a sacredness to the atmosphere. We thought about what brought us to that path as we circled around and around until we got to a large rock in the center. When we got to that rock, we were supposed to place our hand on it and acknowledge someone or something from our story.

As I walked, all I could think about was twenty-year-old Jessica, back when she met Matthew. She had just been engaged in faith for a few years and had met someone who seemed too good to be true. He was nine years older, a good listener, faithful, and kind. Twenty-year-old Jessica was full of light and hope and had not experienced any major pain in her life. She was bright-eyed and innocent, and she never could have imagined what was ahead. Her imagination only allowed for good things and happiness, not ache and loss.

With the hum of the bagpipes ringing in the clearing, I placed my hand on that stone and said, "For twenty-year-old Jessica." And I don't think I've ever held myself with such compassion as in that moment. I didn't hold any judgments, spite, or frustration with my younger self. She did the very best she could with the information she had and with the experiences she had lived up to that point.

It was that light and love and hope that would carry her to when she was thirty-seven and would find out that the man she loved was gay. And she would make the choice to love him still and build a family that was not what she had dreamed of, but was a new type of beautiful. This love was in large part because the love that twenty-year-old Jessica felt was still alive in her heart seventeen years later.

And so I ask you to look back at yourself with tenderness. Look at all of those iterations that you have been, all of the experiences you have had that have led you here. Instead of questioning yourself in a spiteful manner, have compassion. Not *How could you?* but *How could you not? You did your best.*

THE REWIRING

Shortly after my divorce, I undertook a major remodel of my kitchen and dining room. It was something that Matthew and I had talked about for years, but it was only after our divorce when I remained in the house that had once been ours that I finally made it happen. Everything was removed and demolished. Drywall came down, flooring came up, and cabinets came out.

The dining room had crown molding in it. It was pretty but a bit dated and didn't fit the look I was going for with the remodel. So one day, the contractors pulled it down. As it came down, they found something they weren't expecting—wiring. And a lot of it.

The dining room had can lights, and it appeared that they were added at some point after the house was built. The homeowner must have done it himself, and he ran the wiring for the lights along the walls so he didn't have to cut open the drywall. Then, to hide the wiring, he hung the molding over it.

I remember my contractor telling me that it was a fire hazard. He said, "There's no telling when, but at some point, you could have had a fire because of this wiring." Of course, because the wires were hidden, I had no way of knowing.

The story reminded me of my own life and the rewiring work I was doing to make myself healthier. One area was in intimate relationships. Because the unraveling of my marriage had been slow, I found myself pondering the idea of dating just a few months after Matthew had moved out. By that point it had been about a year since he first told me he was gay. I recall Stephanie saying that dating was necessary to rewire the pathways that were broken. These pathways had to do with the way I saw myself and my body, the fears I had around relationships and being left, and the idea that love might never be possible again. Like in my dining room, some of my own wires were hung improperly and were hazardous if I let them remain.

Slowly, as I dated, I came to understand the idea of being rewired. I remember sometimes crying when I was dating someone because I was experiencing so much beautiful newness and growth. Suddenly, I was faced with painful truths about my marriage, which I could only face when compared with the beauty of new love.

When my therapist talked about rewiring, I didn't expect it to be both beautiful and painful. I think I thought of it more matter-of-factly—like I would simply experience new things and that would teach me new truths. But that is not how rewiring works.

In my remodel, I saw rewiring in action. Wires had to be cut, walls had to be opened, and new pathways had to be built. Yes, those wires that were in the crown molding of my dining room worked and the lights went on, but they were not going to work forever. Just because something is functional doesn't mean it is healthy or best.

The same was true in my marriage, which had light and love and things seemed good, but when the walls were broken down, I discovered wires that weren't installed properly. We created shortcuts, and over time those shortcuts caused things to short-circuit or not function at all. We didn't even know what was wrong, similar to how the previous owner of our house thought his work was fine.

One of the greatest gifts we can give ourselves is accepting and embracing the messy work of rewiring. We all have things we were taught or have done to function a certain way, and some of those things are not the way they should be.

Maybe you were not taught how to manage money.

Maybe you never saw healthy relationships modeled for you.

Maybe you stayed in a job that wasn't life-giving because you didn't feel empowered to choose something else.

Wherever you have been, you can rip down the molding, pull down the wires, and start again. It is messy and uncomfortable, but you will find that when it is done, your light is brighter. Your world is safer. Things are better.

It wasn't until the marriage had ended and I was forced to knock things down and rebuild that I could see the flaws that had been there all along. Seeing the flaws, though, made me appreciate the beauty in the new. The rewiring was very necessary, though I couldn't see it hidden behind the molding.

THE GAP AND THE GAIN

About two years after my divorce, I listened to a book called *The Gap and the Gain: The High Achievers' Guide to Happiness, Confidence, and Success*. It is one of those business books you typically see at an airport kiosk. I don't know why I bought the book, but I am so glad I did because the principle was a game changer for me. In the book, the authors explain a mindset where you shift from thinking you are in the gap (lacking in something or something has been done to you) to thinking you are in the gain. They write:

> Being in the GAIN means you measure yourself backward, against where you were before. You measure your own progress. You don't compare yourself to something external... When you're in the GAIN you focus on what you've actually done. You measure your GAINS and use those GAINS to create more and better GAINS in your future.[1]

Essentially, they are shifting the reader's perspective, saying that if you look at things in life happening *for* you and not *to* you, you will be able to heal, grow, and change faster and overall have a more positive outlook on life. Though most of the examples in the book were for people in business, I found it profoundly helpful from a personal perspective.

I know it maybe seems extreme to measure your disappointment in the gain, but as you accept your story and disappointment, I think this way of thinking can be helpful. I know I am able to see gains that I couldn't easily see when I was going through the hard time in my marriage's demise. I wonder, if I had had this perspective, if some things would have changed for me. I catch myself looking at things from a gains outlook and find that it has been transformative.

Consider what experiences you look at as gaps and how you can change your perspective to be a gain. Some of the ways you might frame it include:

I used to see _____ as a gap, but now I see it as a gain because _____.

_____ is a gain because _____.

The gain I have received from _____ is _____.

WHERE DO I GO FROM HERE?

A friend once said to me, "I feel like I am just waiting for the bottom to fall out. I wish I knew what was coming. I feel like my life is going to implode at any moment." I said to her, "But the same could be true if you were in a really good place right now. We never know what is going to happen. The best that we can do is say, 'What can I give to today? How can I accept where I am right now and keep moving forward in a way that makes me proud?'"

We don't get to control a lot of what happens to us in life. But what we do get to control is how we respond and move through our circumstances. We can choose to be people of hope, grace, and compassion. We can actually do the thing we once thought impossible. Moreover, we can thrive in the midst of it and because of it. I know this because I did it.

My husband's coming out could have made me say I'm never going to date again.

My husband's coming out could have made me not trust people.

My divorce could have made me anti-marriage.

My divorce could have made me think I had to stick with a traditional corporate job.

My divorce could have made me think I couldn't travel alone.

But it didn't.

And that is because I said I wanted something more. I will not let this control my life. What happened to me is not going to define me. My grief will not be my story. My story will be one of hope, healing, and betterment of myself. I am proud of myself and the story I have written. And you can be proud of your story, too.

CHAPTER 14

REBUILDING A LIFE
YOU LOVE

I spent most of my childhood years in Oshkosh, Wisconsin, a small city an hour south of Green Bay. Yes, it's the town where Osh-Kosh B'gosh was founded. I attended Oshkosh North High School and was active in numerous clubs, theater, and music groups. Each year the school would honor a former graduate for the school's Hall of Fame. This was someone who had demonstrated excellence in adulthood. I dreamed of someday being one of those inductees. I thought there would be no greater honor than to be recognized by my school and community in that way.

Fast-forward twenty years and one of my favorite former high school teachers, Mr. White, reached out to me. He was coming to Nashville and wondered if I would like to do lunch. I enthusiastically said yes, eager to reconnect and catch up. I took him to one of my favorite Nashville restaurants, and there he told me that I had been selected as the 2023 Oshkosh North High School Hall of Fame recipient. I immediately got teary, as forty-year-old Jessica took in the news that fifteen-year-old Jessica had dreamed of.

It felt especially beautiful to receive the honor after my divorce. I traveled with my three kids to Oshkosh for an assembly of about 1,500 people, including my extended family, former teachers, and a few old friends. I spoke about five actions to be successful. These five points were:

1. **Be persistent:** Grit and determination will get you everywhere.
2. **Be a connector:** Living with open arms and welcoming everyone to the table is always worth it.
3. **Make room for new dreams:** Your dreams are allowed to evolve. Make room for those new dreams.
4. **Love your people:** Loving people well will always serve you well.
5. **Make it rain:** You are the one who makes your success.

As I think about rebuilding a life that I love, I followed the same principles I shared with those high school students. My life looked different than I imagined it would. But it still was filled with much joy, hope, fun, and even love. Over the past four years, my view of love has deepened and expanded. Of course, I have always known there to be many kinds of love.

Love of things that bring delight, like the first peonies of the spring and clean, crisp sheets after a long day.

Love of places. The beach and the ocean make my heart swell. I can't get enough of either.

Love of times and seasons, like as the sun breaks the horizon in the morning, or the chill of a crisp fall day.

Love of a job, of getting to do something that fills me up and brings me joy.

Love of friends, the people who see me and know me.

Love of family, the people I didn't choose and who didn't choose me, yet we love each other fully and completely, no matter what.

Love from a lover, a person who knows every freckle and dimple, every scar and every ache, and who is always, always there.

And most importantly, **the love of self.** This love comes when you know who you are and you are tender with all of the different layers that you have. It is a love that is deeper and more expansive than all the other kinds of love because it is the only love you will have your whole life. It is a love that truly never fails and is always with you. I believe we are wired for love because we are made of love.

Rebuilding a life you love starts with loving yourself purposefully. It is also important to remember that love is not only for people in committed relationships—it is for all of us, every single day. Love is for friends and family. It is for the strangers we meet in the grocery line and the people we follow on social media. Love is one of life's greatest gifts, and we get to live it out, regardless of our circumstances, every day.

Prior to my divorce, I think my view of true love was much more narrowly focused on the intimate love of marriage. I didn't think of it broadly very much, though I certainly threw the word *love* around. I think I thought that my married love and physical intimacy was the ultimate life goal, that somehow that was the most important love to have.

Yes, the love within a marriage is beautiful, and it has its place in many people's lives. But in the shattering and rebuilding, I have found that love is much bigger and deeper than my old perspective. The way we love and allow ourselves to be loved leads to a rich life. Love is something that grows, changes, evolves, dies, is born, and is discovered. So how then do we make love the fabric of our entire life? How do we create a life that we love?

A LIFE YOU LOVE

I want to take some time to unpack the idea of creating a life you love, despite a loss or disappointment. I have seen so many friends go through periods of disappointment and do the hard work of rebuilding. When I was sixteen, my grandma lost my papa, to whom she was married for nearly fifty years, after he got a blood clot from a routine surgery and it resulted in multiple strokes. They had been inseparable for most of their lives, and though her grief was deep, she lived with intention for more than twenty years after his death. She was active in local community clubs, baked for loved ones, and made time for her family. She loved fashion, gardening, and volunteering. Though she missed Papa every day of these twenty years alone, I don't remember her ever not being filled with love and tenacity.

In 2008, my friend Angie and I were pregnant with babies at the same time when her daughter Audrey was given a diagnosis that was incompatible with life. Audrey was born in April and passed away less than two hours after being born. Angie then watched me birth my son a few months later, holding Elias when he was minutes old. I'll never get over how much courage that took. In her pain, she celebrated with me. Angie showed me that no matter the depth of the loss and disappointment, life is worth living and enjoying. She demonstrated the truth of holding two different emotions at once, as she carried her deep grief and true joy over Elias's birth. In the years that followed, we both had additional children, changed careers, moved, and so much more. Angie never let Audrey's death stop her from living a beautiful life.

Throughout this book I have shared lots of principles and practices, and now I want to apply all of those things to one exercise. I used to work in marketing, and a common practice when taking on new clients was to create a SWOT analysis. A SWOT analysis is a chart of four boxes, with one box for strengths, one for weaknesses, one for opportunities, and one for threats. Strengths and weaknesses are internal things, and opportunities and threats are external things.

I want you to take time to do a SWOT analysis for your life, as it is right now and through the lens of creating a life you love.

What are the strengths you bring to your life?

What are the weaknesses you bring to your life?

What are the opportunities you see for your life?

What are the threats you see for your life?

STRENGTHS	WEAKNESSES
OPPORTUNITIES	THREATS

There is no right or wrong way to do this. The point of the exercise is to take a holistic look at your life, because you can create only once you know what you have and what is possible. For instance, if I was going to do this for my life, here are some things I would put in each of the different boxes.

Strengths:
- My kids and I have a great relationship.
- I take good care of myself.
- I have a strong friend group.
- I have flexibility with work.
- I have financial stability.
- I'm confident, motivated, energetic.

Weaknesses:
- My house feels chaotic.
- I say yes to too much and become stretched too thin.
- I sometimes have a quick temper.

Opportunities:
- Dating to find a partner.
- Scaling my business.
- Hiring help to assist with areas of stress.

Threats:
- My work is competitive.
- Kids are growing up!
- Limitations with kids' school schedules.

Once you do this exercise, you might gain a new perspective around what you love about your life and where opportunities exist to improve things. I encourage you to do this without judgment toward yourself. As I have written throughout this book, we are all on journeys of growth and refinement. The only way to create a life you love is by doing the work, a little at a time. Sometimes when an artist is creating a painting, they will find they need different supplies from what they have on hand. Likewise, you might find that as you are journeying toward something new, you might not have all the tools and/or resources that you need. Doing a SWOT analysis can help give you perspective about where you are and where you want to go.

A life you love does not mean a perfect life. It does not mean that you won't have moments or seasons that are tougher. What it does mean is a life that is filled with good people and good things that help you feel happy and whole. Consider the relationships and experiences that bring happiness, joy, love, and peace to your story and lean in to those.

WHAT IT MEANS TO CHERISH

I once told a man I was dating about my desire to be cherished. This really stuck with him, and one day he texted me to tell me that he had been reading definitions of the word, saying that his favorite definition was "to cultivate," the way a farmer breaks up soil so that things can grow. Cherishing means caring enough about something or someone so that growth can happen in places that were dormant or unloved.

Though he was not a good partner for me, I am glad that I saved that text message definition of *cherish*, because I have thought about it a lot. I think the work that I have done myself has been a form of tender cherishing. I have broken up and fed the soil of my heart and soul to allow for new growth to begin. I have watered and tended to that soil. And I am in a place now where I do see new life starting to grow.

In my wedding bouquet, I had stargazer lilies, one of my favorite flowers. Stargazers are bigger than a regular white Easter lily, and they have hot-pink centers and a strong, fragrant scent. I have loved them since I was a girl. In 2017, Matthew planted a stargazer plant on the path going up to our house. I thought it was one of the most tender things at the time.

After we got divorced, I didn't want to have the stargazer growing at my house anymore. It was a reminder of our wedding and the loss of Matthew. One day, I paused when I got to that plant, bent over, and ripped it out of the ground. *There,* I thought to myself. *That feels better.*

The next year, it grew back, and again, I ripped it out. *Please stop growing,* I thought to myself. *You represent a life I don't have anymore.* The next year, the same thing happened. I realized that I was not tending to the plant in the right way. I needed to dig up the soil and remove the roots for the plant to stop growing.

I have found the same to be true in my own life. In life, I think I've tended to certain areas, but then they come back, just like that stubborn stargazer. Tending isn't always a ripping out or away. Sometimes, you have to get out a shovel and really dig, turn over the soil and find the hidden roots. And when you do that, that is when the change and growth you seek happens. That is the kind of cherishing you want for your life.

THE TRANSITION

I can't put my finger on it, but somewhere along my healing journey, I went from feeling like *I thought it would be better than this* to *This is my one beautiful life and I love it.* I went from feeling like I was not going to survive to really thriving. Sure, there are hard moments and hard days, but the overwhelming feeling is that life is better. I am better. I think this is because I had to rely on only myself. Because I had no choice, I stopped relying on a partner to help me navigate life and make choices. When I was forced to go at things on my own, a new rising occurred within me.

I saw an Instagram video of bestselling author Mel Robbins speaking, and she said this:

> The bottom line is no one's coming. No one. No one's coming to push you. No one's coming to tell you to turn the TV off. No one's coming to tell you to get out the door and exercise. Nobody's coming to tell you to apply for that job that you've always dreamt about. Nobody's coming to write the business plan for you. It's up to you. And because you're only ever going to do the things that you feel like doing right now or that feel good right now, unless you understand that you've got to parent yourself, you've got to push yourself, you're not going to make your dreams come true. There's a tremendous amount of liberation that comes when you accept the fact that you're always going to need to give yourself a push.[1]

It doesn't matter if you have a partner or not. We all have the ability to push ourselves enough to say, "I want something better. I am going to work to transition from where I am to where I want to be." Yes, resources, partners, and opportunities can make this more or less difficult, of course. But more than any of those things is the inner desire to push ourselves. Like Mel said, it is liberating.

When I decided to leave my job and become a full-time influencer, I was so, so nervous. One brand that I had been working with for months invited me to do a curated campaign for them. My favorite picks were going to be showcased on their website, and my photo would be on the site and in their social media. It was a very big deal. All the past influencers they had worked with had ten to fifteen times the following that I had. And I remember feeling a bit of imposter syndrome: Why me? Was I good enough? And then I had to shift my thinking, remembering that I had worked hard to be here. I had pushed. My sales numbers proved I *was* good enough. I was not the same creator I had been two years before. I was playing in a different sandbox now. Seeing myself as worthy was definitely part of the transition I had to go through to embrace the opportunity before me.

The same will be true for you. It's like all of a sudden, the scales are not so unevenly balanced. You will see yourself in a new light. You will see your story as something that has shaped you to get to this place. As that happens, I encourage you to take a moment and breathe it in. Take stock of where you have journeyed. Be proud of yourself. Say, *Well done*. I am a woman who got back up again and again, and it was worth it.

ON FINDING HOME AGAIN

A few months after Matthew moved out, I remember standing in the kitchen of his new house, my arms around his waist, with my head tucked perfectly between his pecs, crying. This spot felt like home more than any other place to me. My head had rested there more times than I could count. It was where I always felt safe, loved, and known. I stood there for a minute and then, as tears rolled down my cheeks, I said, "This spot has always been my home. How can I do this? How can I go on without a home?"

He hugged me a little tighter and stroked the back of my head, quietly saying, "I know."

I knew I had a physical home, but my whole adult life had revolved around this man, our love, our family. And to no longer have him as my husband, to no longer be able to land with my head on his chest, made me feel like I was homeless. I worried I would never be loved again. That I would be alone and homeless all the days of my life.

As I started dating, I fell in love with the song "Feels Like Home" by Drew and Ellie Holcomb. If you haven't heard it before, put down this book and play it right now. The song takes listeners on a journey of memories that feel like home, such as Grandma's birthday cake, a Tennessee river in the morning, and a highway sunset. It's got a beautiful melody that always gives me goosebumps and makes me smile.

I thought that if I found a new partner, I would have a home again, one that felt like the words of that song. And you know what? It happened. I seriously dated several men who felt comfortable enough to be a new potential home. While those relationships didn't work, I began to understand that just as we have more than one physical home in our lives, many things can be a metaphorical home for us. Someone else would make me feel loved and secure again. Matthew was my first home, and I loved him with all my heart. Though our marriage was unable to last, that didn't mean that the way I felt at home with him was invalid. It just meant that I had the opportunity to find home again.

But it was after my third serious breakup that I realized I was looking for the wrong thing. I realized that we all have many homes over the course of our lives—not just the physical homes that we live in, but the people who make us feel seen, loved, supported, and safe. If we are lucky, we experience home in a variety of relationships.

I feel at home on my friend's front porch, the fireflies lighting up her yard on a summer night.

I feel at home talking to an old friend I've known since I was eleven.

I feel at home when I sit in a theater, as I was a performer for most of my childhood.

But let me tell you the secret I learned. While all these people and places felt like home, my true home was with none of them. It was with myself. No one can be our home. And when we find home in ourselves, we are able to bring a more whole version of ourselves to relationships and the circumstances that life brings us.

Right after I finished the first draft for this book, I started dating someone new. Early on in the relationship, I had a counseling session with Stephanie. We were talking about how everything felt different about this relationship. She said, "This is the first relationship I have seen you have where you are bringing your whole self and he is bringing his whole self. Neither of you seem to be trying to use the other person to fill something in yourself." I agreed with her. In previous relationships, I was looking for the idea of home in someone else, not sitting in the comfort of myself as my home. I nodded, saying, "Yes, I feel like a new person, and it has changed everything." And experiencing that strong sense of self enabled me to love this man in a richer, more confident way.

I am my home.

And you are yours.

No matter your disappointment, your ache, your sorrow, your loss. You have yourself, and you are home. And that home holds your heart. Treat it with all the love it deserves and lavish that love wildly on all this earth has to offer.

CHAPTER 15

ENJOYING YOUR EVERYDAY

I stopped at a thrift store on the edge of Nashville one early spring day. They were having a closeout sale and everything was $1. Yes, $1. I thought I had died and gone to heaven. People had baskets overflowing with finds. I headed straight for a display with old books on it. One of them was an old sermon book by Thomas De Witt Talmage from 1885.

A few weeks after buying the sermon book, I decided to open it up and read a few pages. Here is an excerpt, which I have thought about ever since I read it for the first time.

> We promise nothing for these sermons except that they are out of the old ruts. The church of today is divided into two parties—the Ruts and the Anti-Ruts. The former are in favor of driving along in just the way that all the proceeding religious vehicles have gone...anything new, in manner or mode, is frightful...But the Anti-Ruts would rather be out than in the old groove. Yet they want to be sure that they are on the right road...They have rougher riding than those who keep in the ruts. The vehicle bounces sometimes fearfully. Obstacles are apt to be thrown in their way.[1]

I read this sermon written 170 years ago and all I could think was, *Wow, wow, wow.* I really identified with the imagery of the ruts in a road, the way we choose to travel, and what life looks like if we travel a different path. In the sermon he goes on to talk about how if someone chooses to travel within a rut, it will be very difficult for them to get out of that rut without breaking the shafts or removing the wheel.

If you are reading this book, you are an Anti-Rut. Not in the religious sense like the preacher was referring to, but in the idea that you are creating your own path. You went through the pain of forging something new, even if it meant breaking. You are not riding in the same paths carved out by your choices or the choices of others around you. I hope that is a visual you can hang on to as you forge your path in the weeks and months to come.

I think one of the biggest challenges of being an Anti-Rut is that you might not have a guide for how to navigate forward. You might not know anyone who has lived this story or gone through this pain, and so the unfamiliar feels terrifying. Or maybe you have seen someone with a similar story, but you want to do some things differently. I am here to tell you that there is no one way to do disappointment.

You get to make the rules. As you move forward and hopefully use some of the tools in this book to create new habits and patterns, you will see change happening.

In Nashville, we have Bradford pear trees everywhere, and in spring, the trees go from barren to gorgeous white in what seems to be a day. Of course, it isn't a day. That work has been going on throughout the long winter and spring. Likewise, you will do a lot of work that maybe no one sees. You might be like those Bradford pear trees, with white flowers of new beginnings about to burst forth. All of a sudden, you are in the spring of your story.

That said, spring usually brings showers, and some days, even amid your blossoming, the thunderstorms may come. I am doing remarkably well, and yet occasionally the grief of my story still makes me cry. Crying is okay. Feeling your feelings is okay. I have learned that grief is a part of me now, and it always will be. My heart has grown to love myself and others more deeply and to accept the scar tissue of grief. Grief doesn't disappear, but it does become much more manageable.

Remember that just because you still feel disappointment doesn't mean you aren't growing and making positive changes. Don't let hard feelings or setbacks prevent you from continuing to move forward. You control your outcome, so stay focused on doing that work and forging that path.

MARKED BY BRAVERY

A year after I got divorced, I met a photographer on a bridge. I was wearing a leather jacket and a black tank top. I handed her a tube of red lipstick and said, "Can you please write the word *brave* across my chest and then take my photo?" I wanted to document that moment in time. A moment when I felt both shaky and brave. A moment when I knew I was changing, growing, and coming into myself. I wanted to see myself as the world saw me.

Brave was a word that was said to me again and again after my divorce. "You're so brave," people would say. I struggled to believe what they said. A lot of the time, I didn't feel brave. I felt heartsick, deep sorrow, confusion, pain, exhaustion, grief. Some weeks felt like I was just getting through the next hour, the next day, the next week. The unfamiliarity of being alone after having been married for basically my entire adult life was incredibly difficult.

But somehow, despite the sadness over my marriage ending and the unknown future, I began to see myself the way the world saw me: brave.

Brave to start over.

Brave to learn love in a new way.

Brave to make our home *my* home.

Brave to pursue a dream of entrepreneurship.

Brave to not let sorrow be my whole story.

Brave to share.

Brave to love myself with intention.

Brave to say, "This is not the end."

A week later, I got the photos back from the photographer. The series of images took my breath away. There I was. A woman marked by bravery. A woman who was not only just making it, but making things new, better, and stronger than before.

Someday, twenty years from now, when my kids are grown and I'm a grandmother, I want to tell the story of my bravery. I will tell them how I kept showing up for myself and how God held me in the palm of His hand. That I was never alone because of Him, because of my family and friends, because of my community. I was never alone because I found a companion in myself.

The definition of *brave* is "ready to face and endure danger or pain; showing courage."[2] I don't know that I could have ever been ready for my story to unfold the way it has, but I am grateful for my strength, integrity, compassion, and *bravery* to live well. Living brave doesn't have to mean jumping out of a plane or fighting in a war; it can also mean showing up for yourself and those you love amid hardship.

Today may you look at your own story and acknowledge when you have been marked by bravery. What you are walking through is likely painful, difficult, sad, frustrating, and exhausting. The act of getting up again and again and working to change is inherently brave.

Of course, it sounds neat and tidy at the end of the book to say, "Yay, look how far we've come! We've done it!"

Life is not like that. This is not a two-hour movie. I still have days when I cry. I still have days when I wish life were different. I still have days when I don't feel strong or brave. The same will be true for you.

But I know this: many days I am happier than I have been in years. I feel more like myself since my divorce, which is strange to admit because when I was married, I didn't not feel like myself. I think because I went almost directly from college to marriage, I didn't take time to really learn to listen and act on the small voice within myself. I didn't acknowledge to myself or my husband what I wanted and needed. Despite my divorce, my life is full of goodness, light, and love, and I couldn't be more grateful.

The truth is, when someone asks how I did it, the answer is I didn't have a choice. Matthew is gay. We couldn't remain married. I cherish that Matthew remains a close friend and safe place for me and my kids. But life is different from how it was. He and I are now walking on different paths, though they often come back together. I think when you are forced to do something, you surprise yourself.

I surprised myself the first time I drove to Wisconsin.

I surprised myself with that first post-divorce kiss.

I surprised myself by managing a remodel.

I surprised myself by leaving a secure job to work for myself, without a spouse's income to fall back on.

When you have no choice, you do one thing and another and another. Eventually, you realize life is all about not knowing how to do something and doing it. And the more you do, the more you feel comfortable with uncertainty. It gets easier and better.

YOU ARE WORTHY

Have you ever thought about your own worthiness and what that really means? *Worthy* is defined as:

1. having adequate or great merit, character, or value: *a worthy successor.*
2. of commendable excellence or merit; deserving of one's time, attention, interest, work, trouble, etc.: *a book worthy of praise; a person worthy to lead.*[3]

I love the second definition for you and me. We are worthy of time, attention, interest, work, and trouble. Yes, we are. Worthiness isn't for someone else who is wealthier, smarter, prettier, or more fit. It is for all of us.

You hold the keys to this. You must believe deeply that you are worthy. Because when you believe in yourself, you change your life. Your self-worth is directly tied to how you will live in this world. I hope that after reading this book you can more confidently say, "I am worthy of living a story that I am proud of. I am worthy of a life of hope, dreams, and opportunities. I am worthy of every good thing." Because you are. And holding on to that belief will get you further than any other act.

You matter. Your story matters. Your passions and dreams matter. And if you have learned anything in this book, I hope it is that you bring value to the world and that it is never too late to start again, start over, or simply start. You might have thought that life would be better than this, and guess what? It still can be.

HOW TO STEP FORWARD

As you endeavor to step forward and make choices to redefine your circumstances, find courage and hope, and live fully, remember these key principles:

- **You are enough.** You have everything inside you that you need to step out and make the changes you want for your life. You are enough, so don't let doubts tell you otherwise. Don't get distracted by what you see on social media. Stay laser focused on what you are seeking, and know that with your courage and drive, you can do this.

- **You have control.** You have the ability to own your story, so do that. Embrace the messy and make the changes necessary to create the life you want given your circumstances. Only you can do it, so take control and the steps needed to move ahead with purposeful intention.
- **You can do hard things.** Whatever you are facing, it is not easy. But easy isn't worth fighting for. And you have already proved to yourself that you can do hard things, so lean in and do the hard work. It will be worth it.
- **You are worthy.** You are worth fighting for. You are worth trusting. You are worthy of the dream you have for your life, and you get to seek it out. Don't let doubts and lies poison your mind. Lean in to the truth of worthiness. Fight for it and your dreams.
- **You must keep going.** Sometimes you are going to want to quit. You will want to say that you can't do it, it's too hard, or it isn't worth it. Those are lies. You must keep going. Because someday, you will be able to look back and see all you have accomplished, and you are going to be so proud. You have the pen to write a new chapter for your life—don't stop now.

Remember that car deodorizer I mentioned buying in 2020? For four years, it hung on my rearview mirror. Its brilliant turquoise-and-floral pattern faded, but its powerful message—"Not to spoil the ending, but everything will be okay"—did not. Four years later, I decided it was time to take it off my mirror. I no longer needed the daily reminder that everything will be okay because everything *is* okay. I am okay. My family is okay. My life is okay. In fact, in a lot of ways, it is way better than okay. It is wonderful, beautiful, happy, and safe. Jessica in 2020 wasn't sure it was possible, but Jessica in 2024 can't get over the wonder of how her life has healed, evolved, and been made new.

Your reading this book shows me that you are about to live out your redemption story, because redemption doesn't happen when we sit on the sidelines. Redemption happens when we move forward despite pain, sadness, and unmet expectations. You, too, will be okay. When you take the proverbial bull by the horns and decide to live differently, you will change your life.

I know because I did it. And I believe you can, too.

ACKNOWLEDGMENTS

To Angie, Ann, Chelsea, Chris, Colleen, Courtney, Janssen, Jen, Joy, Linda, Lysa, Mallory, Meg, and Mike, who sat with me as I cried and cheered me on as I healed and then soared—I'll never forget your loving kindness. The richness of your friendship is one of the greatest gifts of my life.

To the women who participated in focus groups, read my earliest drafts, and provided helpful feedback, I humbly thank you. And to my trusted friends who read draft after draft and pushed me to dig deeper, get more vulnerable, and tell richer stories. A special thanks to my friend Jonathan. I really don't think I could have done this without you. You made this book better.

To the men I've dated since my divorce, thank you for teaching me something about myself. I will be forever grateful for the dinners, the stories, and even the heartbreaks. A special thanks to Justin and Jerry, who have remained kind friends.

To Onsite and the friends I made there, thank you for holding space for me to be vulnerable, grieve, and grow. You changed my life.

To Stephanie, my dear therapist. The way you have held space and gently guided me during the past five years has been so sacred. I will never be able to thank you enough.

To my beloved online community, you truly are the best people on the internet. This book is for you. Thank you for every message you've sent me—from your brokenness in your own stories to your kind encouragement. I have carried each one with me as I wrote this book, and I hope you felt seen in these pages.

To my team at Worthy Publishing, especially my impeccable editor, Beth, thank you for believing in this book. Your encouragement has been life-giving, and I feel so grateful to be a part of your publishing roster.

To my agent, Andrea, thank you for catching the vision for this book from its earliest stages and always advocating for me. Your friendship with our family for nearly twenty years is a treasure.

To my assistant, Sara, who helped ensure I was present online when I had to focus on this project. Your encouragement lifted me up on more days than you'll ever realize. I am so grateful we get to work together every day.

To John, whose daily presence and laughs throughout this project's editing phase brought me so much joy. Brick by brick, you've changed my life. I cannot get over the grace of you.

To my parents, Debbie and Rick; my sister, Melissa; Aunt Sandy; and all the family whose endless belief in me has strengthened me on the hardest of days, I love you.

To Matthew, who has loved me since I was twenty years old. There is no one I would rather have as a co-parent. Thank you for your bravery and love of our family. Also thank you for all the ways you have loved me since our divorce—from killing spiders to cutting my grass to listening to me cry on my hard days—I don't know what I would do without you.

To Elias, Adeline, and Ezra, you have lived this story. I hope someday you look back and are so proud of our family and the way we have loved one another and grown. You are the most remarkable humans I know, and being your mama is the greatest joy of my life. I love you more.

NOTES

CHAPTER 2

1. Sarah Mae, host, *The Complicated Heart Podcast*, season 1, episode 21, "Processing Trauma with Counselor Adam Young," April 24, 2019.
2. "What Is Trauma?" Crisis House, July 12, 2022, https://www.crisishouse.org/post /what-is-trauma.
3. Edith Shiro, *The Unexpected Gift of Trauma: The Path to Posttraumatic Growth* (Harvest, 2023), 20–21.
4. Bruce D. Perry and Oprah Winfrey, *What Happened to You? Conversations on Trauma, Resilience, and Healing* (Flatiron Books, 2021).
5. Jeanne Stevens, *What's Here Now? How to Stop Rehashing the Past and Rehearsing the Future—and Start Receiving the Present* (Revell, 2022), 103.
6. Tom Percival, *Ruby Finds a Worry* (Bloomsbury Children's, 2019).
7. Liane Hansen, *Weekend Edition Sunday*, "Yellowstone Fires: Ecological Blessings in Disguise," September 14, 2008, NPR, https://www.npr.org/2008/09/14/94534548/ yellowstone-fires-ecological-blessings-in-disguise.
8. Mike Mariani, *What Doesn't Kill Us Makes Us: Who We Become After Tragedy and Trauma* (Ballentine Books, 2022), 309.

CHAPTER 3

1. Brené Brown, *Atlas of the Heart* (Random House, 2021).

CHAPTER 4

1. Anne Lamott, "Age Makes the Miracles Easier to See," *Washington Post*, January 17, 2024, https://www.washingtonpost.com/opinions/2024/01/17/age-acceptance-love -hate.

CHAPTER 5

1. Robert D. Enright, *Forgiveness Is a Choice: A Step-By-Step Process for Resolving Anger and Restoring Hope* (APA Lifetools, 2001), 28–29.
2. Jeanne Stevens, *What's Here Now?* (Baker, 2022), 79.
3. Aaron Lazare, *On Apology* (Oxford University Press, 2005), 45.

4. Enright, *Forgiveness Is a Choice*, 78.
5. "Forgiveness: Letting Go of Grudges and Bitterness," Mayo Clinic, November 22, 2022, https://www.mayoclinic.org/healthy-lifestyle/adult-health/in-depth/forgiveness/art-20047692.
6. Kevin Queen, Cross Point Church, Nashville, Instagram reel, January 9, 2024, https://www.instagram.com/reel/C15dNdjqrDH.

CHAPTER 6

1. Richard Paul Evans, *The Four Doors: A Guide to Joy, Freedom, and a Meaningful Life* (Simon and Schuster, 2013).
2. Bronnie Ware, *The Top Five Regrets of the Dying: A Life Transformed by the Dearly Departing* (Hay House, 2019).
3. Brené Brown, "Dare to Lead List of Values," https://brenebrown.com/resources/dare-to-lead-list-of-values.
4. Jesús González, "Water Also Has Feelings—Masaru Emoto," Medium, September 25, 2023, https://medium.com/@jesuglez15/water-also-has-feelings-masaru-emoto-460104472dae.
5. Shauna Niequist, *I Guess I Haven't Learned That Yet: Discovering New Ways of Living When the Old Ways Stop Working* (Zondervan, 2022).

CHAPTER 7

1. "Our Epidemic of Loneliness and Isolation: The U.S. Surgeon General's Advisory on the Healing Effects of Social Connection and Community," US Public Health Service, 2023, https://www.hhs.gov/sites/default/files/surgeon-general-social-connection-advisory.pdf.
2. Juana Summers, Vincent Acovino, and Christopher Intagliata, *All Things Considered*, "America Has a Loneliness Epidemic. Here Are 6 Steps to Address It," May 2, 2023, NPR, https://www.npr.org/2023/05/02/1173418268/loneliness-connection-mental-health-dementia-surgeon-general.
3. Robin Dunbar, *Friends: Understanding the Power of Our Most Important Relationships* (Simon & Schuster, 2013), 203.

CHAPTER 8

1. *The View*, "Jennifer Lopez on What She's Learned Through the Years," September 12, 2019, ABC, https://www.facebook.com/watch/?v=527873841302806.
2. John Stamos, *If You Would Have Told Me: A Memoir* (Henry Holt, 2023).
3. Travis Bradberry, *Emotional Intelligence Habits* (TalentSmart, 2023), 113.
4. Jamie Kern Lima, *Worthy: How to Believe You Are Enough and Transform Your Life* (Hay House, 2024), 9.
5. Christine Comaford, "Got Inner Peace? 5 Ways to Get It Now," *Forbes*, April 4, 2012, https://www.forbes.com/sites/christinecomaford/2012/04/04/got-inner-peace-5-ways-to-get-it-now.

CHAPTER 9

1. Jamie Kern Lima, *Worthy: How to Believe You Are Enough and Transform Your Life* (Hay House, 2024), 98.

2. Ashish Sharma, Vishal Madaan, and Frederick D. Petty, "Exercise for Mental Health," *Primary Care Companion to the Journal of Clinical Psychiatry* 8, no. 2 (2006): 106, https://www.ncbi.nlm.nih.gov/pmc/articles/PMC1470658.
3. Wayne Muller, *Sabbath: Finding Rest, Renewal, and Delight in Our Busy Lives* (Bantam Books, 1999), 101, 143.
4. Mark R. Rosekind et al., "The Cost of Poor Sleep: Workplace Productivity Loss and Associated Costs," *Journal of Occupational and Environmental Medicine* 52, no 1 (January 2010): 91–98, https://pubmed.ncbi.nlm.nih.gov/20042880.
5. Danielle Pacheco and David Rosen, "Best Temperature for Sleep," SleepFoundation.com, updated March 7, 2024, https://www.sleepfoundation.org/bedroom-environment/best-temperature-for-sleep.
6. Sara Moniuszko, "White Noise to Help You Sleep? A Neurologist Explains Why People Are Turning to 'Sound Masking,'" CBS News, August 25, 2023, https://www.cbsnews.com/news/white-brown-pink-noise-help-sleep-neurologist.
7. Arianna Huffington, *The Sleep Revolution: Transforming Your Life, One Night at a Time* (Harmony, 2016).

CHAPTER 10

1. James Clear, *Atomic Habits: An Easy and Proven Way to Build Good Habits and Break Bad Ones* (Avery, 2018), 64–65.
2. Charles Duhigg, *The Power of Habit: Why We Do What We Do in Life and Business* (Random House, 2012).
3. Alex Kerai, "Cell Phone Usage Statistics: Mornings Are for Notifications," Reviews.org, July 21, 2023, https://www.reviews.org/mobile/cell-phone-addiction.

CHAPTER 11

1. Julia Cameron, *The Artist's Way* (Tarcher, 1992).

CHAPTER 12

1. Pierre Teilhard de Chardin, *The Making of a Mind: Letters from a Soldier-Priest, 1911–1919* (Harper & Row, 1961), 57. Often shared in the form of a poem titled "Patient Trust."
2. Kate Bowler and Jessica Richie, *The Lives We Actually Have: 100 Blessings for Imperfect Days* (Convergent Books, 2023), xix.
3. R. A. Emmons, J. Froh, and R. Rose, "Gratitude," in *Positive Psychological Assessment: A Handbook of Models and Measures*, 2nd ed., edited by M. W. Gallagher and S. J. Lopez (American Psychological Association, 2019), 317–332.
4. Emmons, Froh, and Rose, "Gratitude."

CHAPTER 13

1. Dan Sullivan with Benjamin Hardy, *The Gap and the Gain: The High Achievers' Guide to Happiness, Confidence, and Success* (Hay House Business, 2021), xxvii–xxviii.

CHAPTER 14

1. Mel Robbins, Instagram reel, January 30, 2024, https://www.instagram.com/reel/C2uVra2AexY.

CHAPTER 15

1. T. De Witt Talmage, *Series of Sermons*, vol. 1 (New York: Funk & Wagnalls Company, 1885), vii.

2. "Brave," Oxford Languages via Google, July 20, 2024, https://www.google.com /search?q=define%3A+brave.

3. "Worthy," Dictionary.com, July 20, 2024, https://www.dictionary.com/browse /worthy.

I THOUGHT IT WOULD BE BETTER THAN THIS

READING GROUP GUIDE

DISCUSSION QUESTIONS

Reading *I Thought It Would Be Better than This* would be a powerful experience for friends, small groups, and book clubs. Use the questions below to help facilitate meaningful conversation.

Jessica loves to join book clubs via Zoom whenever possible. Please reach out through her website if you are interested in having her say hello to your group: JessicaNTurner.com/BetterThanThis.

CHAPTER 1

What is your *this*?

Discuss a time when you went through a both/and moment.

CHAPTER 2

How did Jessica's reframing of trauma to include *What happened to you?* shift your thinking (if at all)?

Have you ever thought about fire as being helpful? In what ways has the fire in your story been helpful to you?

Jessica shares four tactics for moving through pain—acknowledge it, talk about it, comfort yourself, and pray. Which of these tactics resonated with you and why?

Are you someone who struggles with staying present? If so, how did Jessica's story inform why that is a helpful practice?

CHAPTER 3

Have you ever been afraid to speak up about something hard in your life? What helped you to stop holding it in?

What has your experience been with therapy? Was it helpful?

What is a time when sharing your experience helped someone else?

CHAPTER 4

If you have gone through grief, what was helpful during the hardest periods?

On pages 52–53, Jessica shares three lies about grief. What lies have you believed?

What strategies about grief resonated with you? Have you tried any of them?

CHAPTER 5

On pages 66–67, Jessica shares what forgiveness isn't. Have you ever believed the "not" statements she shared?

Share a time when forgiving someone was healing for you.

Have you ever found it difficult to forgive yourself? What did you do to overcome those feelings?

Did you do the 360-degree examination of your life? If so, what did you discover?

CHAPTER 6

How do you feel about the word *control*? Do you agree with Jessica that you can regain control over parts of your life?

What is a longing you have for your life that you have not acknowledged or shared with someone?

On pages 86–88, Jessica offers three exercises for articulating the dreams for your life—the "What I Want" chart, the vision board, and the values assessment. Which of these was most helpful and why?

How was being a student of your disappointment helpful?

CHAPTER 7

Do you ever feel lonely? What stood out to you about the loneliness epidemic in America?

What are ways you invest in friendship in your life?

What makes it challenging to invest in friendship?

CHAPTER 8

Would you say you love yourself or you are working on falling in love with yourself?

Have you ever struggled with loving your body? If so, what has been challenging?

What are ways you care for yourself?

What do you think about the concept of worthiness? Do you believe you are worthy of good things?

CHAPTER 9

Have you struggled with unhealthy habits during times of disappointment?

What ways do you incorporate movement in your days? Do you struggle with this or find it easy to prioritize?

During busy seasons, do you find it tough to rest and get enough sleep? If so, what strategies are helpful for making this attainable?

How did you score on the report card at the end of the chapter?

CHAPTER 10

What new experiences have you had after a disappointment or season of grief?

Did you take the personal inventory of your habits on page 151? What stood out to you?

What would you include on an experience bucket list?

CHAPTER 11

What creative practices do you find life-giving?

If you struggle to know what creative practices you would enjoy, what discovery suggestions that Jessica provided were helpful? Did you do any of them?

Jessica wrote about trying pottery and while she struggled, it was a positive learning experience. Have you ever tried a new creative outlet and struggled with it? What did it teach you?

Are you a journaler? If so, what form of journaling do you practice and what do you enjoy about it?

CHAPTER 12

What spiritual practices do you have in your daily life?

Share a time when you asked someone to pray for you and how it made you feel.

Share the blessing you wrote for your current season.

Name three things you are grateful for right now.

CHAPTER 13

In what ways have you accepted your circumstances and how has this acceptance made things easier?

How do you look at your younger self? Do you struggle with judgment of her or are you able to look at her and her situation with compassion?

What is an area of your life that has been rewired and how has that affected you?

CHAPTER 14

What is your view of love? Did the different types of love that Jessica shared resonate with you in any particular way?

Share about the SWOT analysis exercise and what it showed you.

Jessica talks about discovering that she is her home. How did this section make you think? Did you have any aha moments?

CHAPTER 15

What new path, like the Anti-Ruts, are you creating for yourself and your life?

Jessica did a photo shoot with the word *brave* written across her chest. What word would you write across your chest?

Jessica shared five principles for stepping into your next chapter. Which one stood out to you and why?

ABOUT THE AUTHOR

Jessica N. Turner has spent the last two decades as a content creator and tastemaker for busy moms looking for hacks to live life with more intention and less stress. Additionally, Jessica is an award-winning content strategist and marketing professional. She speaks at events nationwide on a variety of topics including work-life balance, grief and disappointment, and social media best practices. She is also the author of the *Wall Street Journal* bestselling book *The Fringe Hours: Making Time for You* and *Stretched Too Thin: How Working Moms Can Lose the Guilt, Work Smarter, and Thrive*. She has been featured in numerous media outlets including the *TODAY* show; the *Tamron Hall Show*; *O, the Oprah Magazine*; *People* magazine; *Better Homes & Gardens*; Time.com; Inc.com; and more. Jessica lives with her three children in Nashville, Tennessee. Connect with her at JessicaNTurner.com and on Instagram at @JessicaNTurner.

JOIN JESSICA N. TURNER AND ONSITE CLINICAL DIRECTOR RYAN BLOCH-SNODGRASS FOR AN EXCLUSIVE FREE COURSE:

What now? Practical steps to navigate disappointment and learn to dream again.

Visit experienceonsite.com/betterthanthis